33

The Private Life
of a Country House

THE PRIVATE LIFE
OF A COUNTRY HOUSE
1912–1939

Lesley Lewis

ALAN SUTTON

First published in the United Kingdom in 1980
by David & Charles (Publishers) Ltd

First published in this edition in Great Britain in 1992 by
Alan Sutton Publishing Ltd
Phoenix Mill · Far Thrupp · Stroud · Gloucestershire

First published in this edition in the
United States of America in 1992 by
Alan Sutton Publishing Inc · Wolfeboro Falls · NH 03896–0848

British Library Cataloguing in Publication Data

Lewis, Lesley, *1909–*
  The private life of a country house
  I. Title
  942.676

  ISBN 0–7509–0080–6

Library of Congress Cataloging in Publication Data

Applied for

Line drawings by Stephanie Harrison
Endpaper illustration: Pilgrims' Hall, *c.* 1960

Typeset in 10/12 Bembo.
Typesetting and origination by
Alan Sutton Publishing Ltd
Printed in Great Britain by
Billings, Worcester

Contents

ILLUSTRATIONS

To Barbara and to the memory of Bill and Joyce,
the brother and sisters with whom I shared
my home

FOREWORD

Since the first publication of my book in 1980 there are inevitably, and sadly, changes to record. My younger sister, Joyce, died later in that year and my brother, Bill, in 1987, both very suddenly while in full vigour. Only Barbara and I, both now widows, survive from the family which grew up in Pilgrims' Hall. The death, in April 1991, of Bill's widow Evelyn, brought the dispersal of many things which were arranged in their house and used much as in my parents'. Barbara's two children and seven grandchildren have now taken over most of these possessions, some of which, if not antiques in my time, have now become so. Some fine pieces of period furniture, which under modern conditions could not be properly cared for at home, have been put into safer surroundings. The 'Garrick' cabinet, which I inherited, is at Temple Newsam, while the satinwood bureau, commode, armchair and Chinese dragon, also from the drawing-room, the red lacquer clock from the hall, and the Chippendale mirror from the dining-room are in Pitshanger Manor, Ealing. There they will be seen in settings of appropriate scale and character. The Chinese fan has gone to the Fan Museum, Greenwich.

The Christian fellowship which bought Pilgrims' Hall in 1968 is now named after it, and continues there as a widely connected centre for teaching Bible history, caring and renewal. It has extended generous hospitality on occasions concerning my family, thus preserving links with the past and a much-valued friendship.

My father and brother meticulously kept household accounts over many years and although these are not in themselves important they may in time, by collation with similar material, contribute something to social history. These therefore have been given to the Essex County Record Office together with some other papers and a small collection of books on Essex accumulated by the family. As I stressed in my book, my home was utterly typical of many flourishing in England in the early twentieth century, but as their memory grows dimmer I hope these domestic details are of sufficient continuing interest to justify this new presentation.

Lesley Lewis
November 1991

THE PRIVATE LIFE
OF A COUNTRY HOUSE

THE FAMILY

I am going to write about my home as I can remember it in the years from about 1912 to 1939. It was then quite an ordinary one and indeed was typical enough of the minor English country house, its equipment and routine. Give or take some idiosyncrasies, the little less or little more conservatism in taste, the little less or little more money, countless families like mine lived in these houses much as we did, unselfconsciously and anonymously. It is more difficult to find period examples of everyday wear than costumes for grand occasions and in the same way detailed records of such households may well become scarce once they have passed out of living memory. Any systematic retention of papers would indeed at once make them atypical and if my mother referred to something being 'in the archives' she meant she had irretrievably lost it, thus hiding for me the true meaning of the word.

Families like mine rarely kept diaries of any general interest, they tore up their letters and, perhaps not wholly guilelessly, they covered their tracks with remarkable efficiency. Transient love affairs, even the sweetly harmless flirtations which never progressed as far as christian names, could tarnish reputations in a manner now inconceivable, and discretion was by far the better part of romance and indeed of life in general. They often forgot to label portraits and miniatures, and although senior relatives reminisced copiously they could seldom be pinned down to any firm facts. They did not seem to remember details of what must have been relatively dramatic events. Surely when my maternal grandfather lost his small fortune in a Glasgow bank smash, and his wife hers in a family brewery, there must have been some kind of dénouement, some realization of how their lives would be changed, and indeed were changed, but no, they rarely mentioned the matter.

For them, no croquet boxes full of priceless papers, no drawers full of forgotten Elizabethan needlework, no references in the memoirs of the famous. Moving house fairly often, they cleared up as they went, got christened, married and buried wherever they happened to be and, regarding themselves as essentially private people, would never have imagined their doings could be of interest to anyone but the immediate family, who would know it all anyway. They thought it illbred to claim any importance for themselves, and the females of the species wonderfully complicated their syntax by habitual use of the pronoun 'one', going to almost any lengths to avoid the first person singular, that unspeakably egotistical one-letter word 'I'. They were not so much undramatic as anti-dramatic and could kill incipient scenes or embarrassing revelations with a meaning look or a remark so devastatingly irrelevant that the protagonists hardly knew what had hit them. Therefore I will respect the privacy which was so lovably and essentially a part of them, and only say enough about people to explain the things we used. Before the 1914–18 war eroded, and the 1939–45 one virtually destroyed, the whole system of domestic service and social habits which supported and was supported by the upper-middle-class way of life, there were numerous objects and procedures which now make no sense at all. Once it ceases to be used for its original purpose some standard article may quickly become incomprehensible, and I am going to try and recall what we had in our house, and what our normal routine was in an era which has become remote in so much more than mere time.

Most professional families of some substance must have had from time to time a few participants in great affairs, some original personalities, some contacts with the famous, some interweaving of public and private life, though not enough to draw them out of the latter. We probably had an average share of distinctions and celebrities. My father's family was a legal one and his maternal grandfather, James Bacon, was a Vice-Chancellor, a notable character in his day, a man of some literary talent with an agreeable gift for drawing and a bone-dry wit. Our paternal grandfather was a solicitor in an established Lincoln's Inn firm to which in due course he contributed his name as senior partner, and my father, James Lawrence, followed him into it, as did my brother. Among my father's first cousins were the foundresses of a famous girls' school, and his youngest sister, Susan, was among the first women Members of Parliament. Notwithstanding these formidable examples or perhaps, I have sometimes thought, because of them, my father did not think much formal education necessary for his daughters. With my sisters I was taught at home by governesses until at the age of seventeen I went to a finishing school of high social repute run by the three Mesdemoiselles Ozanne – Marie, Alice and Lydie – at 4 Avenue Octave Gréard, Paris VIIIème. I was really too green for such sophistication but, to their eternal credit, the Ozannes enabled me to do what I naively thought was the only object of the exercise, and to learn French with a thoroughness which still surprises me.

My maternal grandfather, William Pott, was a soldier, a younger son of a Border family whose devotion to games and field sports may have had something to do with the loss of their property. However, my mother's four sisters and four brothers, though never happier than when in each other's company, made a wide circle of friends, led satisfactory lives and created charming homes whether in India, or with the Navy or wherever they might be. A characteristic which they shared with my father's more intellectually-inclined relations was a natural discrimination in the choice of everyday objects, so that we were brought up to handle and live with things which were good of their kind though only accidentally and occasionally collectors' pieces. My mother, Kathleen, living on in our family home until she was ninety-two, preserved a continuity in which many of the old ways, and the corpus of family possessions, survived into a period in which they had become something of an anachronism.

On my return from Paris at the age of eighteen I did what my neighbours and contemporaries did if their parents could afford it – hunted when there was a horse to be had, played tennis, went to dances and stayed in houses which for the most part were run like ours. I did my stint in local good works such as the Red Cross, helped wherever help was needed at home and at all odd moments read voraciously. Ultimately my studious tastes gained over my athletic, sporting and social ones and I persuaded my father to let me try and matriculate by means of a correspondence course, in order to go to the recently founded Courtauld Institute. On the verge of the 1939 war I had London University degrees in the history of art, some literary and lecturing commitments, a modest job as registrar of the City and Guilds of London Art School, and was living in London. The outbreak of war took me back to live at home, travelling daily to Lincoln's Inn to work as a stopgap managing clerk in the family firm for four remarkably happy and strenuous years.

Although of course we did not know it at the time, my sister Barbara's wedding in 1932 really marked the peak of our corporate family life. After that we all began rather more to go our separate ways and the benevolent hold which our home had over us came to feel perhaps somewhat restrictive. At the age of twenty she married Ralph Sewell and went to live about six miles away at Ingatestone, setting up a household which was a rather smaller replica of our own. They had a cook, parlourmaid, housemaid, gardener and a groom, and in due course an old-fashioned nanny for their boy and girl. Meals were served to them in the dining-room amid the traditional panoply of silver and glass, and I am sure it was not till the war came that my sister ever thought of cooking anything herself.

The new ménage was magnificently launched with a wedding in what was then the absolutely standard form for a family like ours, with about two hundred and fifty guests of all ages. There was a great gathering of really very elderly relations, some of whom we of the younger generation had never seen before and probably never saw again. Either fewer were still extant when my next sister got married or it was thought that the conventions had been sufficiently honoured by asking them to the first wedding. As it was October there were some rather old-fashioned long fur coats about and female dress varied from the frankly dowdy to the height of the current fashion. Country weddings were occasions for which to buy new clothes and really to make a great effort about one's appearance, so that photographs taken at the time must, to a costume expert, date them exactly. The men wore the virtually unchanging uniform of black tailcoat with black top hat, except for a few dashing grey ones, a pale waistcoat, striped grey and black trousers and sometimes white or drab spats. The latter seemed to disappear after the war, perhaps because of their skilled and expensive workmanship. A few frock coats, reaching to the knee all round, were still to be seen but except for senior clergy they had become rare. The bride's long white dress, train and veil, with sprigs of orange blossom, were strictly orthodox and all of us six bridesmaids, whether children or grown-up, had pale apricot georgette frocks with yellow velvet jackets and sprays of autumn leaves. We wore the crystal necklaces which were the bridegroom's present to us and our satin court shoes were dyed to match the dresses, something you could always get done at one of the big London department stores.

The day was the culmination of many weeks of strenuous activity which involved the employment of dressmakers, the buying of

Bridesmaids at Barbara's wedding, autumn 1932. Standing: Hermione Pott and Dawn Watson, cousins of the bride, with Craven Charrington, the bridegroom's nephew. Seated: Sally Womersley, friend, Lesley and Joyce, the bride's sisters, and June Charrington, the bridegroom's niece

Joyce's wedding, 1938. Gerald Chamen and Joyce with D'Oyley Sheppard, the best man. Sally Womersley, Gill Charrington, David Bedford, friends; Richard Sewell, the bride's nephew; June Charrington, friend; Tom and Mary Quennell, the bridegroom's nephew and niece

Guests at Barbara's wedding, 1932

Aunt Edith Gordon Clark, Aunt Emily Pott, Uncle Stanley Gordon Clark and others at Barbara's wedding

numerous clothes, the ordering of luggage which would have my sister's new initials stamped on it, the booking of a caterer and discussion of his arrangements. A copper plate, about four by six inches, was engraved for the invitations, ordinary printing for this purpose being considered rather vulgar. Most people replied promptly but there were a few black sheep and those of us who had tackled the list with some levity got into hot water with my father when he found we had very little idea of how many were actually coming. By burning the midnight oil, however, we came up with a reasonably accurate count at the end. According to convention everyone who was invited was likely to send a present, even most of those who could not come. They poured in thick and fast with a good many duplicates but very few were of a basically useful kind. A large stock of house-linen was provided by the bridegroom's family and such major items as table silver and china were mostly given by near relations after prior consultation. There was an extensive trousseau with much hand-made underwear although the vegetable artificial silk called milanese or celanese had made its appearance by now so that ready-made pants and slips could be bought.

The miscellaneous presents were such things as sets of coffee cups, fruit glasses and bowls, crystal water-jugs and decanters, thermos flasks of all shapes and sizes, coffee-making machines, items of silverware, flower-vases, paperweights, inkstands and pen-trays, tooled leather blotters and stationery-cases, ashtrays of glass or metal, cigarette-boxes in expensive materials such as silver or shagreen. Other popular items were trays, especially those of painted wood decorated with coloured prints protected by glass or varnish, table-mats, bookslides, cocktail shakers, lamps and lampshades, some rather terrible. Pictures tended to be conservative, water colours or sporting prints, and the sporting theme was also taken up in shooting sticks and carriage rugs. There would be a few pieces of furniture, mainly smallish items such as looking-glasses, fire-screens and oc-casional tables. Clocks were in considerable variety, antique and contemporary. Among all these things there were of course a few ugly and tasteless ones, offset by gifts of imagination and originality such as a piece of old china or a beautiful book. The donors were all thanked by the happy couple before the day or the gift was acknowledged by someone else if they had got behindhand with their letters.

This glittering array of objects was of course quite valuable and had to be watched over by a detective when it had all been set out for display on the billiard-room table. Inspection of the presents was a very interesting and enjoyable part of the entertainment and the families concerned thought much about their arrangement. One had to resist the temptation to classify them and put, say, all the thermos flasks together. The feelings had to be spared of friends who had given duplicates, triplicates and even quadruplicates, and you distributed such gifts as far apart as possible. Every present had to have its appropriate card attached, usually a visiting card with suitable inscription, and any accidental mixing up of these added to the high tension of the whole proceedings and produced panic quite disproportionate to its cause.

The pattern of weddings then was much the same as today except that because of some technical detail of licensing or registration the actual marriage had to be completed by 3 pm. This made for a certain pressure if the ceremony was in the afternoon, as it usually was, and there was nothing social about luncheon which the bride was likely to have on a tray in her room. The service in the parish church was the same then as now, the bride's father bringing her along when everyone else was assembled and leading her up the aisle with veil down. Emerging from the vestry with the bridegroom she threw it back from her face for the walk down the church. The couple, parents and bridesmaids would then take a flying start to get to the house and line up to receive the guests who piled into their cars and followed as best they could. Parking had not then reached the sophistication it has today, the lanes near country churches were in their pristine unwidened state and cars and drivers were far more idiosyncratic than now. At any kind of large party there were always incidents to be sorted out by outdoor staff and local constables, these being recounted for months afterwards with great enjoyment and losing nothing in the telling. We had no room big enough to hold everyone at once so the house itself was used as an approach to a marquee erected over the terrace and entered through the french windows. There, after the formal greetings, the guests drank champagne, ate the delicious canapés, sandwiches, ices and éclairs provided by the Mayfair Catering Company, and inspected the presents in the billiard-room. The cake was cut and toasts drunk but without the speeches which later became customary, and also without anyone reading out those disastrously facetious telegrams some people could not resist sending. Then, the day being reasonably fine, much of the party spilled out into the drive for more casual enjoyment, the time going so quickly for all except perhaps the bride and bridegroom that the festivities seemed hardly to have started when they drove away towards their Mediterranean honeymoon.

When my sister Joyce married another near neighbour, Gerald Chamen, in April 1938, everything was much the same. There were probably a few useful fireproof dishes among the presents but as yet none of the saucepans and pots and pans which would soon be introducing wartime brides to a lifetime of cooking. My father, whose health had beeen deteriorating for some time, died a few months later, in January 1939. My brother and I were working in London, I was only home at weekends, and the household was scaled down to my mother's lesser requirements pending any radical decisions about the future of the house. The war settled the matter for us with ten evacuee children billeted upon us, and although they were moved to a safer area before the Battle of Britain was fought over our heads, there could then be no question of moving. So it was that my mother continued to live at Pilgrims' Hall until 1968, even reviving after the war something like the old ways, with daily domestic help and rather rapidly changing cooks who alone lived in. In March 1942 my brother married Evelyn Townsend, our friend since childhood, and after the war and his army service ended, settled in a house two miles from my mother's. In 1944 David Lewis, whose father had been rector of the neighbouring parish of Shenfield when we were young, came on leave from the Sudan and married me. I went back with him to eleven years in the tropics, waited on by male Arab servants who, from the days of Kitchener, had absorbed much of the household lore which in England had mostly been forgotten. In our own home, on Nile steamers, in the bush where we seldom failed to dress for dinner, we ate delicious steak and kidney pies or plum duff, regardless of the climate.

When we returned to live in London in 1955 I was still almost as innocent of domestic know-how as I had been when I left but, coming in at this advanced post-war phase of mechanization, I found it not too difficult to pick up enough to enable us to do without much outside assistance. In 1968 Pilgrims' Hall was sold to a Christian training centre and is kept full and busy, with croquet still played on the lawn, ponies in the fields and more young voices to be heard about the place than ever before. Long may it flourish under its new name of Fellowship House and leave with its occupants a pleasant memory of big light rooms, tall trees casting long shadows on the grass on summer evenings and a garden which still has some wild places in it to kindle the imagination. I contemplate my old home without nostalgia for it seems irrelevant to one's life today and I can hardly recognize myself in its obsolete routine. Yet it was rich in human interest and warm personal relationships, and I affectionately dedicate this book to those old friends whose crafts and skills maintained the decorum of my home.

Two

MY FIRST HOME

My parents married in 1906; my brother Bill, their eldest child, was
born in 1908 and I in 1909, so I have only a few memories of the house
we left in 1913. The move, however, was a watershed event for me,
for dating things before and after it. The first house was called Warley
Side, on the green of what was then a country village near Brentwood
in Essex and about twenty miles from London. We used to emerge
first in one perambulator and then in two, after Barbara, the elder of
my two sisters, was born in 1912. The prams were shallow and
boat-shaped, riding high on curved springs over two large and two
small narrow-rimmed wheels with tyres of solid rubber reinforced by
an internal wire, which could be seen when they wore out and fell off,
causing a mild sensation to the nursery party. There were hoods to put
up in wet weather by means of a jointed brass brace, and if it was
extremely hot a fringed white canopy was rigged instead. Whatever
the elements we were always most securely protected against them; in
winter I wore a white rabbit fur coat with bonnet to match, and Bill a
white fur with little tails to imitate ermine and a similar round fur cap.
The original pram was painted dark green with black lines, the colours
adopted by my parents for their carriages and liveries. The second
pram was dark blue with red lines, lent by an aunt whose children had
outgrown it and, perhaps because of the alien colours which Nanny
was rather snobbish about, the nurserymaid always had to push that
one. Our two attendants wore dark grey serge or tweed coats and
skirts, or costumes as they called them, with plain black hats, felt in
winter, straw in summer. The skirts were long and full and a familiar
accident was the catching of a heel in the braid with which the hem
was turned up, very annoying for them as it involved sewing a new

9

piece of braid round the two yards or so of a full skirt. Their dress hardly seemed to change over the years.

Our twice-daily walks had plenty of incident with many friendly encounters. Everyone was on foot, horseback or bicycle or in a trap, and most were ready to exchange greetings. The village had several rather older families than ours, in the grander houses, so our arrival was probably welcome. My parents' landlord was Evelyn Heseltine, a rich philanthropist, who had built the elaborate and, I now see, very beautiful Art Nouveau church at Great Warley in which three of us were christened and to which Bill and I were taken on such special occasions as harvest festivals. The church was then quite new and the rush-seated, high-backed chairs in our nursery had been sold off from the old, inconveniently sited one which it replaced. Just down the road from us was Mr Coe's forge. We used to watch him and his men working the bellows to make the coals glow, and then holding a red-hot iron rod on the anvil and hammering it turn by turn, in perfectly timed strokes, until it became recognizably a horseshoe. At intervals they would plunge it into a bucket of water, making a sharp hiss and lots of steam. They would punch nail holes in the red-hot shoe and then hold it briefly against the hoof to test the fit, producing a sizzle and a whiff of burnt horn. Finally the shoe would be cooled and nailed on, the horse's bent leg being held firmly between the blacksmith's knees. Probably if the horse was restive we were not allowed to stay, so this fascinating operation comes over with a cosy feeling of harmony between all parties in the marvellous fire-lit cavern. Mr Coe was my first hero and when they suggested getting him to extricate me when I idiotically got my head stuck between the bars of my iron and brass-railed cot, I wrenched it out agonizingly over my ears to avoid such an indignity.

Deliveries to the house were all made by horsedrawn vehicles, each with its own character. The butcher had a spanking bang-tailed cob and a very smart shiny green trap adorned with lots of polished brass. He had a waxed moustache and in summer wore a straw boater above shirtsleeves, waistcoat and striped blue and white apron, of which one corner was tucked up through a tape round the waist. He carried the meat into the house in what looked like a miniature stretcher, hollowed from a block of white wood, and beautifully clean except for fresh blood. Then off he went again in a tremendous hurry, cutting corners and spraying up the gravel of the unmetalled road. The milkman, also in a striped blue apron, was more leisurely. His quiet half-clipped pony drew a low-slung cart which had a large brass-banded churn standing in it, with cans and a long-handled measuring dip hanging at the sides; he would dip the milk from the big churn into quart or pint cans, made of bright silvery-grey metal with a dropdown wire handle and a lid on a triangular brass hinge. The baker was different again. He had a full-sized horse and a covered van with a rear flap, through which he took out the bread on open trays, so that there were delicious smells of hot horse in front and hot bread behind. Fish, of which we ate a lot, was not delivered, but fetched from the fishmonger's open marble slabs in the local town to the big zinc-lined icebox in our larder.

On the ground floor at Warley Side were drawing-room, dining-room, small passage-room, kitchen, pantry and, rather oddly, a large coach-house. The back door, which the nursery party always used, was cut out of the big one opened only for the carriages or car. Over the coach-house was a long room where the maids slept, as in a kind of dormitory, and round the side of the house were the stables. These no doubt were out of bounds to us at our tender age but I remember one occasion of great jollity when the carpets were hung on a line there to be beaten with special racket-shaped implements, made of interlaced split bamboo, which brought out clouds of dust. The grooms helped the maids and it was not only the carpets which were swiped at. We hardly ever went into the dining-room, being much too young to have meals there, but it was dark, I remember, as I think most dining-rooms were then, and over the chimney piece was a picture of a ship in full sail. It was the first painting I ever consciously noticed, and on the same occasion I observed my father, reading his paper. Fathers in those days were fairly detached, not to say sheltered, from their offspring, and I had not really taken mine in as a person till this moment at the age of about three, when I had a good look and thought 'that's him'.

The drawing-room is more easily remembered because its contents were removed bodily and arranged in almost exactly the same way in the 'boudoir' of the new house. There was a glazed corner-cupboard with china figures in it, sofa and armchairs covered in a mainly green and white floral chintz, an elegantly inlaid writing-table

Bamboo carpet-beater

Warley Side, my first home

with chair to match, and a revolving bookcase which must not be twirled round at speed because the books fell out. An urn-shaped silver lamp and a white china cupid one lit the room, and on small tables were some little enamelled or silver boxes which opened in various ingenious ways. A gilt clock with a pair of doves on top gave out a faint rapid chime. The carpet was green, with some Persian rugs here and there. The whole room was probably in perfect taste for an Edwardian bride and furnished almost entirely with pretty new things, my parents as yet having neither inherited nor bought the antiques which they later preferred. The fittings of the desk were particularly fascinating, with silver inkstand, pen-tray and pens, silver-cornered Russia-leather blotter and a little cut-glass bottle with

a silver lid incorporating a brush for moistening stamps and envelopes. Russia-leather was dark brownish-red, criss-crossed with diagonal stamping and giving off a faint delicious smell, rather like cedarwood pencils.

Our domain was the nursery with its big hanging iron lamp, kept carefully trimmed by Nanny, a bright fire behind a high brass-edged fender secured to the wall by hooks, and a fluffy brown hearthrug on which I was sprawling with a book of nursery rhymes when I first discovered that I was reading by myself. We only went to the front of the

Ivory and silver-gilt French eighteenth-century étui

house by appointment, as it were, and in the morning my mother gave us lessons. All I can remember is that she scattered on the floor the cardboard letter-squares from a game called 'Wordmaking and Wordtaking' and told us to arrange them like the words of a page of the fat red *Reading Without Tears*. We did learn totally without tears I think, except for those induced by the last story in the book, which we had to read for ourselves as my mother would not face it. It was about a family going for a picnic with a donkey-cart, and all getting drowned when the tide came up. We did not mind about the mother and children, very unappealing in bonnets and shawls and frilled pantaloons which seemed silly for a seaside outing, but it was terrible about the donkey. Sometimes the routine was broken by my mother practising on us the bandaging she was learning at Red Cross classes. She used a triangle of white cloth, covered with mysterious diagrams in blue, but it was probably meant for much bigger patients and the results never felt very firm.

At 6 pm, after nursery tea, we would be dressed up for a further drawing-room session in which starch played an unwelcome part. I had a white dress of broderie anglaise – fine cotton or lawn with a pierced and embroidered floral design – and a pale pink silk ribbon sash worn high over my not inconsiderable stomach. Not till later was this kind of thing replaced by the soft wild-silk Liberty smocks in green or blue, hanging more flatteringly from the shoulders. My underwear then and for several years afterwards consisted first of combinations, wool in winter, cotton in summer. This curious garment was perhaps less bulky than separate vest and pants, but as no one ever did up the buttons at the seat it was both indecent and draughty. Over this came a sleeveless bodice of quilted cotton to which suspenders were attached when you graduated from white ankle socks to black woollen or white cotton stockings. Then there were white cotton drawers with banded and frilled legs, very prickly, and a waist-length cream flannel petticoat, its edge beautifully embroidered by Nanny, in scallops with a dot in the middle of each. For guidance when doing this she had paper transfers with the design on them and ironed them off so that the dots and scallops appeared as blue lines on the cloth. Over this was worn a stiff white cotton petticoat, drawn up round the neck by a narrow tape which had to be tied. It was difficult to dress oneself as nearly everything fastened at the back, but some independence could be achieved by doing things up in front and turning them round afterwards. Anything put on inside out, however, had to be kept that way all day because it was said to be terribly unlucky to change it, a rule I still feel it very rash to defy. My ordinary indoor shoes were round-toed, of soft leather, but the evening ones were more elegantly tapered, bronze-coloured with very thin soles, and kept on by narrow elastic crossed on the instep.

My brother had stouter shiny black patent-leather shoes with bright silvery buckles. He suffered perhaps even more than me from starch, because he had to change his daytime striped sailor blouses, with accessories attached, to stiff white ones which had separate blue cuffs attached to the sleeves by links. We were instructed that his black silk scarf, folded and then tied at the back of the neck, was mourning for Nelson and that the three lines of white braid on the square collar commemorated the victories of the Nile, Copenhagen and Trafalgar. This was confusing because, belonging as we did to a horsy family, we were apt to hear first of historic events and characters as the names of horses, and the one on which our silver Duke of Wellington sat was Copenhagen. By day we hardly ever went out without hats, mine a fluffy so-called beaver felt or in summer a much-beribboned straw confection. They were kept in place by an elastic under the chin and this if smartly snapped by a hasty grown-up caused a peculiar agony which brought tears to the eyes. I envied Bill his straw sailor hat, turned up all round, and his round cap adorned with the name of our naval uncle's current ship embroidered in gold on a black ribbon.

Among other mysterious names were those of the foxhound puppies 'walked', that is to say boarded and exercised, for most of their first year by staunch supporters of the local hunt. This was the Essex Union of which my mother's uncle, Edward Mashiter, was Master for many years. The puppies were not treated as pets, since this might have spoilt them for their future life with the pack and, much as we loved domestic dogs, the slobbering tongues on a level with our faces and the over-boisterous greetings repelled rather than invited affection. At the annual Puppy Show, a function of excruciating tedium to me, my parents would receive a pair of teaspoons engraved with the names of that year's puppies. I still have those for Chaffinch and Chataway, 1915, and I sometimes wonder if the names on such spoons, of which there must have been a great many in circulation, ever cause mystification in antique shops today.

The staff at Warley Side consisted of a butler, Langridge, dressed in tailcoat with striped or black trousers; a houseboy, Harry, in a grey suit and very enviable stout boots with tags sticking out at the back; a

Kathleen Lawrence at Warley Side in about 1911. She is driving a mare, Lassie, in a smart green dogcart. This had no protection from the weather but was the parents' favourite conveyance, which they drove themselves

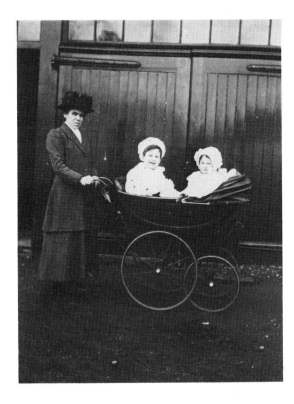

Bill, three, and Lesley, two, being taken for a winter outing by Nanny, whose grim expression belies her benevolence. Both children wear white rabbit coats and hats, Bill's having black spots to imitate ermine

The staff at Warley Side, 1913. Back row: Fred Trickett, head groom, with his terrier, Trixie. He was killed early in the First World War, and she pined, a little white ghost in the stables; then Dolly, house-parlourmaid, who later married a chauffeur; Langridge, the butler, in the traditional dress of an evening tail coat over daytime waistcoat and trousers; Simmonds, the chauffeur, displays well-polished crested buttons on the plastron front of his dark green livery; Chris, undergroom, wears his best suit. Second row: Fanny, housemaid, in her afternoon uniform of black dress and starched apron, but without her cap; Maude, the cook, has a pale print dress under her apron; Nanny, holding John, the house terrier, wears an all-enveloping white apron over her blouse and dark grey skirt; Lucy, the nursery-maid, with Joey the cat, probably had a bright pink or blue dress under her apron; Frank, second groom, indicates his calling by a white stock with his best suit. Harry, houseboy, is sitting in front, tidy and demure

Swanage, 1913: Lesley and Bill in smocks, pictured with a younger friend. Hats were always worn on the beach for fear of sunburn and the smocks and paddlers left little bare skin

head groom, Trickett, in tweeds and leggings, cloth cap or bowler, who put on a dark green overcoat and black top hat if he acted as coachman; two undergrooms, Chris and Frank, and a gardener, Fewell. Then, on the female side, Maude, the cook; Fanny, the housemaid; Dolly, who doubled as parlourmaid and assistant housemaid; Nanny Rapley and, when Barbara, my next sister, arrived, Fanny's sister Lucy as nurserymaid. Nanny wore a woollen skirt and choker-necked blouse all day, putting on an apron for such jobs as bathing the baby. The nurserymaid and others worked in pretty cotton dresses in stripes and colours usually faded from much laundering, wore starched white aprons all the time and sometimes starched white caps. Dolly and Fanny changed into black dresses with more decorative caps and aprons for working later in the day in the front part of the house, and the nurserymaid put on a blouse and a coat and skirt for walking us out. They all wore black stockings and black shoes.

Just before we moved to another house we acquired a dark green Austin landaulette and a chauffeur, Simmons, was added to the staff. He wore a green cap with shiny black peak, a thick green cloth jacket with high collar hooked at the throat, and bright buttons with our stag crest on them, green breeches and highly polished black leggings and boots. Cars needed a lot of attention in those days and certainly he mended many punctures, ringing the hole in the tube with a well-licked purple indelible pencil before sticking a patch on it. He drew well and sometimes elaborated the mark into a horse's head for our benefit. Probably he was less fully occupied than the other men and he often let us hang about him, asking endless questions to which he returned jokey and sometimes cryptic answers. When he went to the war he sent us postcards from France; I got a beauty, a muslin envelope embroidered with flowers and the allied flags, attached to embossed white cardboard and, for good measure, tucked into the flap was a tiny card with 'My love is for you' on it.

Dearly as I loved the chauffeur, however, his car was torture to me for I suffered from acute travel sickness in any vehicle but an open trap. The drab cord material with which the interior was upholstered had a particularly nauseating smell and the windows, which let up and down on a strap, were stiff to open. A little bracket held two cut-glass bottles, one for eau-de-cologne and one for smelling-salts, a survival from the days of vapoury ladies who felt faint, which our relations never did, seemingly. A flexible, silk-covered tube was clipped near the righthand passenger, for communication with the driver, but this was seldom used. Tapping on the glass partition, putting your head out and speaking through the window was more satisfactory. The car held two or, rather squashed, three people on the back seat, and two little seats could be let down facing them. The front seat beside the chauffeur was seldom used.

Our other covered transport was little better from my point of view. It was a brougham, a one-horse carriage inherited from my father's bachelor uncle, Judge Frank Bacon, and rather cramped if there were more than two people in it. It was stuffy in a different way from the car, but stuffy all the same. I used to fix my eyes on the back buttons of the coachman's coat, seen through the little front window, as the waves of nausea rolled over me and sometimes broke. I preferred our grandmother's victoria, drawn by a pair of horses, bigger and nearly always open since it was in the summer that we stayed with her. It had the additional diversion of a footman on the box beside the driver. He let down a folding step for us to get in by, shut the door smartly and clambered aboard as the carriage started to move. This custom of the footman, or coachman if the owner were driving, getting on to the moving vehicle, died hard in some quarters. We used to see the ex-coachman of an elderly neighbour hopping along with one foot on the running-board to get into the spasmo-dically advancing two-seater motorcar driven by his intrepid mistress.

My parents' own favourite conveyance was a high green two-wheeled dogcart in which, apparently perched rather precariously, they drove themselves, unencumbered by children, luggage or attend-ants. The one most in use, however, was the tubcart or governess-cart, with a squarish, round-cornered body and cloth-covered seats along the sides. You got in by a little low rear door with an iron step, and the reins passed over a brass rail on the front. The sides of the trap were painted in broad black and green stripes and, unlike the brougham, it carried no crest. The driver sat in the righthand rear corner, near which was the leather socket for the long whip, used for gentle guidance or removing flies rather than for speeding up. As practised by my parents and our grooms, at any rate when we were with them, the art of driving, and indeed it was an art, was a very uneventful affair, and I never remember anything remotely approa-ching an accident. With them, no horse ever bolted from a too-loose rein allowed to get under its tail and clamped there to the utter ruin of all control. The trot, kept up for long periods, was at a pace of about six miles an hour. Our longest drive would be to a great-uncle, about eight miles away, and anyone big enough got out and walked up the few slight hills. We were in close communication with the roan cob, Lady Gay, and her ears moved constantly to hear what was going on inside and to anticipate orders. She knew perfectly well when there was a train to be caught and if my father was driving her to the station she would trot out smartly with the bell on her collar jingling in fast time, but she never hurried with the nursery parties.

In 1913 we moved to a larger house, Pilgrims' Hall, on the far side of the local town, Brentwood, at a similar distance of about two miles from it. A great deal was done to make it ready for us and we had lovely summer days picnicking in the new garden, out of range of the building operations. The head groom and Nanny, both in a kind of holiday mufti, took us over in the tubcart, chatting companionably over our heads with unusual and welcome disregard of what we might be doing. He wore a straw boater attached to his back collar stud by a black cord hatguard, and she a rather lighter blouse than usual without a coat. We particularly appreciated a huge deodar tree, the lower branches of which formed a dimly lit green tent, softly floored with leaf-mould, but it unfortunately died soon afterwards. A monkey-puzzle tree, the first we had seen and of great interest, was cut down and the formal beds of red geraniums were turfed over, but the fascinating pampas grass, with its waving plumes and the leaves which cut your fingers, survived for another forty years. From the autumn, when we moved in, my memories are all of the new house in which we grew up and where Joyce, my second sister, was born in 1916 to complete our family of four.

Three

THE NEW HOUSE

Pilgrims' Hall was approached by a short rhododendron-lined drive off a not very important main road leading to Ongar and north Essex villages. The solid oak front gates, terminating the quarter-mile or so of oak paling screening the home fields from the road, usually stood open. They were closed, however, on local market days, when cattle might get in and trample the garden, and on Sundays until our frequent comings and goings in motor cars made this inconvenient. A lighter, railed, back gate gave access up another drive to the stable yard and back door, and was used by staff and tradesmen. A four-roomed single-storey white lodge with a central chimneystack stood between the two drives and was occupied by the butler and his family. There was apparently no historic foundation for the name of the house itself but the nearest village was Pilgrims' Hatch, associated with the ancient route between the holy places of Bury St Edmunds and Canterbury, and probably there had been a gate or hatch across what had originally been common land. The village was spoken of as 'the Hatch'.

Our house had originally been a modest three-bayed, two-storey block built in the early nineteenth century and adorned with a wrought-iron veranda, roofed in copper with a leafed edge. Old deeds in the Essex Record Office show that only a few years later bow-fronted wings were added on each side, converting it into a typical Regency country house. The date 1806 on the bell under a charming little cupola may provide a clue to the house's origin and also to the tradition that there had been a chapel in it. The builder or an early occupier was a Roman Catholic priest with the exotic name of Emanuel Dias Santos and this would probably have been enough

18

grounds for a legend, vigorously contradicted and eventually dispelled by my parents, that we were haunted by a headless monk. Certainly nothing was ever seen or heard of anything like this in our time, and the house was bright and sunny, facing approximately south. On the east side there had been some old service quarters which my parents rebuilt as a third bow-fronted wing set back from the main front. Unlike the older part of the house, which only had two storeys, this had three, with a dairy, larder and servants' hall on the ground floor, a day- and two night-nurseries on the first, and four maids' bedrooms above. To the east of the central front door of the main block was the dining-room, with pantry and kitchen behind it, and best spare-room and dressing-room above. On the west was the drawing-room, with smoking-room and billiard-room in line behind it, and my parents' bedroom, bathroom and dressing-room, and 'pink' spare-room and dressing-room over them.

Although little more than a century old when we went there, the house had been altered and changed hands often, being at one time a boarding school, attended by the husband of Mrs Beeton of cookery-book fame. The central block had been gutted to make a large entrance and staircase hall, and this was handsomely panelled in oak. A veined grey marble chimneypiece in the smoking-room may have been original but the others in the principal rooms, as well as cornices and doorcases, were of Adam character and had been imported by ourselves or our predecessors. The drawing-room had a pretty ceiling in low-relief plasterwork applied *in situ* by Italian craftsmen when my parents moved in. My mother used to describe how they modelled the garlands freehand.

The result of all the adding and conversion was that the externally regular architecture concealed curious corners, odd little flights of steps, and excrescences for bathrooms and lavatories which readily froze up. The front and east walls were of white-painted brick, the rest red. In due course, however, the old front crumbled and had to be rendered in cement, a less hospitable base for the Banksia rose, the honeysuckle and vine which thenceforward were somewhat tamed. My parents' alterations were considerable and their architect was Horace Farquharson, evidently a follower of Lutyens. His new wing was excellent but I am not sure he did well to formalize the immediate surroundings of an unpretentious house with so much masonry. He built up the carriage sweep to the front door and made a forecourt enclosed by a brick and stone balustrade, from which semi-circular steps led down to the lawn. Extending beyond the drawing-room bow-window he built a pergola on square brick piers with heavy wooden superstructure, over one end of a flagged terrace on to which the french windows of all the rooms on the west side opened. At the north end of it was a loggia in which my parents sometimes had breakfast, until the family party got too big. Steps led from the terrace down to an Italian sunken garden. This had two square pools, lined with narrow bricks, and in the centre of each was a charming little bronze fountain, one a boy with a dolphin, the other a cherub. These were turned on to play on special occasions or when it was exceptionally hot, creating a summer sound which echoes in the mind's ear. Beyond an outer low brick wall was a small wood, full of snowdrops, primroses, daffodils and bluebells in spring, and concealing an old thatched summerhouse of tarred boards, adorned by criss-crosses of artistically rustic logs.

Mr Farquharson perhaps idealized his patrons somewhat and imagined cultured and elegant guests having tea on the terrace, admiring the sunken garden and appreciating the aesthetics of the fadeout into the cleverly contrived mystery of the dark little spinney. We must rather have let him down because nothing like this ever seemed to happen. Chilly winds blew round to the terrace from the north and on the days when it would have been warm enough the guests, cultured and elegant as some at least may have been, were far more given to playing tennis on the lawns in front of the house. The Italian garden was where we children usually played, sailing toy ships, catching, though returning at evening, numerous newts, frogs and toads, and being gently initiated into some of nature's more brutal aspects by the ferocious habits of the dragon-fly larvae. It was here that at ten years old I met my future husband, of similar age and hopelessly addicted to ponds and their fauna.

Although Pilgrims' Hall never aspired to grandeur, I am interested now to see how, in such houses for the minor gentry, ideas had percolated down from really stately homes. All the elements were here reproduced in miniature. A screen of mixed timber – oak, elm, lime, horse-chestnut – had been planted, probably when the house was first built, all round the eight acres or so of the two front fields, and the first of these was always called the 'park' by village people and the staff, though woe betide us children if we did likewise. At the far end of it but in view of the house was a big deep pond, which possibly stood for a lake though its prime purpose was for watering horses and

Bill, Barbara and Lesley at Pilgrims' Hall soon after their arrival there in 1913. They are sitting in the Italian garden in front of the new pergola

The new rose-garden at Pilgrims' Hall in about 1930

Lesley, at about five, learning to ride on Pedlar, with Bill, beside mother, waiting his turn

Grandfather with Aunt Emmie Pott in their GWK car outside Springwells, Steyning, about 1917. The engine was at the rear and a dickey seat could be pulled out behind it, overhanging the wheels precariously

cattle, a shallow drinking place being railed off for them. In the field were three carefully placed groups of a horse-chestnut and fir planted together, and a remarkably fine Turkey oak stood by itself and bore on its spreading branches a platform for us to play on. We called it the Crows' Nest, painted a skull and crossbones sign for it, and used to act out a pirate game here. Near the house were about eight Spanish chestnuts, evidently all planted at the same time and in most years producing a fine crop. If Capability Brown or Humphry Repton recognized their own ideas in this careful landscaping they might perhaps have been pained at the straight horizontal lines of lower branches, always nibbled just as far as they could reach by the cows and horses grazed in the 'park'. The second field was not ornamentally planted and was often laid up for hay, but it was good for cowslips and mushrooms, which by no means grew everywhere. To a small child it was far enough away for a visit to it to be something of an event and made for a special purpose. This was the only place I remember where I made cowslip balls by hanging the flowerlets on a piece of string which was then tightly tied for me, or pulled the head of one daisy through the split stalk of another one until I had a daisy chain.

The back drive led to a large, square, gravelled stable yard. On one side was the coach-house, with big green sliding doors and, in front of it, a tiled area with glass roof under which cars and carriages were washed. This was done simply with cold water, squirted under strong pressure from a rubber hose attached to a brass tap, highly polished as was all the brass always. A special long-handled curved brush was used for the spokes and the water was dried off with a chamois leather, producing a magnificent and very durable polish. All the time they were doing it the men hissed through their teeth as they did when grooming the horses. Near the tap stood boots for paddling about in the streams of water. They were really just the fronts of boots, with feet attached to thick rigid soles, and legs of stiff leather, thigh-length, fastened at the back with straps over breeches or trousers. There was a light ladder, about eight feet long, with leather-padded ends, for reaching the tops of carriages and cars.

At right angles to the wash was what had probably been the original stables, in yellow brick. Now there was only one loose box, the others having been given over to coal storage, and it was inhabited by Prospero, the obliging brown horse who pulled the brougham but was not above the mowing machine and the farm cart. He was shared between the head-gardener's department and the grooms', a tricky situation which was perhaps relieved by his occupying this neutral ground away from the hunters. The rest of the building contained an engine and the rows of batteries which it charged for the electricity system. It was run usually twice a week, or less in the summer until we rather precociously installed a refrigerator in the late 1930s. The man who looked after the engine, Albert Murrant, was of about my mother's age and, as under-coachman to her eldest sister, had driven her to a Surrey church for her wedding. During his war service he became something of a mechanic and when he came to us he used to decarbonize or 'decoke' the car, run the electrical system and, with an undergroom, look after what horses remained and drive the car. To start the engine, which ran on oil, he would prime it by means of a blowlamp. When it got suitably hot he would swing the big flywheel which drove the belt, and the spokes of the bright brass governor would cease to stand distinct, blurring as the speed mounted. It worked beautifully and may be working still, as we sold it after getting on to mains electricity just before the 1939 war. It was a substantial piece of machinery, bedded solidly in concrete, and it gleamed from polishing and its slight film of oil. Apart from light and, in summer, the refrigerator, it could power only one plated breakfast heater for the dining-room, used on Saturdays and Sundays when we might be late. This had no automatic control so the last comer had to be sure to turn it off before it and the dishes on it became red-hot. There were some wall plugs for lights only and from these one was inclined to get mild electric shocks.

A third side of the yard was enclosed by a range of loose boxes which opened on to a brick-floored corridor. At one end was the chaff room, with a really lethal chaff-cutting machine which we treated with the utmost respect and were allowed to turn on wet days. Hay was moved along a sort of trough and chopped by a blade on a big wheel with a handle. Some trusses of hay always stood near and more could be let down through a trapdoor in the floor of the loft above. This had a door at first floor level, below which a cart could draw up to deliver the fodder and the straw for bedding. Along one wall of the chaff room was a bin divided by partitions, for oats, crushed oats, bran and linseed. These were measured out into sieves or buckets by means of round wooden utensils. Several buckets were kept near the tap and the seldom-used pump over an old well. Four were of wood, painted dark green outside, white within, and banded with iron. They were kept full of 'chilled', or rather unchilled, water for the horses to drink as they might get colic if given it straight out of the cold tap. The four loose boxes had small high windows which the horses could not see out of, and were entered from doors in the wooden partition along the corridor. This had rails at the top, through which the occupants could be seen, and each box had an iron manger in the corner and a rack for hay fixed to the wall at a convenient height for the horse to pull at. The floors, tiled with a gully for drainage, were deeply covered in straw except for one period, presumably of shortage, when bracken was used instead.

At the other end of the range was the tack room with the iron and wooden 'horse' on which the saddles were put for cleaning, a bracket on the end holding the bridles. It was a bright cheerful little room, its red-tiled floor and plain wooden surfaces kept cleanly scrubbed amid all the muddy work which was done there. Its characteristic smell was compounded of saddle soap, metal and boot polish, and tobacco. Most of the work was done standing at a high bench under the window, but the room had one kitchen chair on which the men occasionally relaxed to read the popular daily newspaper which usually lay about. We were, of course, not so very much younger than the boys who came straight from school at thirteen or fourteen, did odd jobs in the stable and garden and learned their craft under the men. We therefore had much in common on such subjects as bicycles and their accessories, tools, electric torches and the sideshows at local fêtes – coconut shies, rifle ranges, bowling for the pig, and so forth – about which they could give us useful tips. The tack room indeed was a kind of club, in touch with all the comings and goings about the back door, and much the least strict of the heads-of-departments' dens.

Out of this opened the harness room which had a coke stove but was little used for working in. The mustard-coloured horse rugs, with braided initials, were kept here in a big mothproof chest. Saddles and bridles, after cleaning, were placed on brackets on the planked walls, while stirrup-irons and bits were hung in a glass-fronted wall cupboard. Stainless steel for such things had not yet become general, so rust was a problem and they were burnished with a five or six inch square of chain mail. Above these rooms and the stables were attic bedrooms and a messroom for the three grooms of early days, who were all unmarried, but I never entered them during the short period in which they were fully occupied.

On the fourth side of the yard were four new loose boxes, built by my parents when they first came. For the horses their great advantage was that the doors opened straight to the outside, not on to a corridor, so that the top halves could be left open for the occupants to put their heads out, see what was going on and be talked to. They would neigh hopefully to passers-by, and on Sundays, after church and before lunch, my parents always visited the stables with any guests who might be there, and we were shown how to offer sugar on a flat palm with thumb tucked in so as not to get accidentally bitten. A groom would be there to trot out a horse to test soundness after the previous day's hunting and a specially interested guest for whom the rugs were removed would slip the groom a small tip. Looking back, this routine seems to have gone on for ever, but we moved house in the autumn of 1913 and war broke out in August 1914, so that only for one hunting season did my parents have their stables full, the car and chauffeur, grooms, horses and traps all kept busy. In the late summer of 1914 we saw from the nursey window three khaki-clad officers ride into the yard on unfamiliar high-cantled saddles over red cloths, with swords and spurs jingling. After a short colloquy more soldiers arrived with horses which were put into all spare stables and, to our delight, two charming officers, Captain Hodges and Lieutenant Scott, were billeted in the house. They must have been horse-gunners, perhaps the local yeomanry, because they exercised guns and gun-carriages round one of our fields and my brother got a ride on one but I, younger and of the wrong sex, did not.

These happy days were all too short. After perhaps a fortnight they all went away, our own hunters were taken for the army through something called 'Remounts', the grooms, chauffeur, butler, and footman soon went too, and an unaccustomed quiet set in. The car and the high dogcart were laid up for the duration and an older man came as coachman to drive Prospero in the brougham or Lady Gay in the tubcart. Matching, my father's heavyweight hunter, was broken to harness and put to work on the home farm, where he caused a sensation by successfully jumping a large fence with the cart behind him. My mother's favourite mare, Tinkerbell, was first lent to the Hunt, and then sent back to us to breed from. She did indeed, on the day of the Zeebrugge raid in 1918, produce a foal, perhaps rather unfortunately named Vindictive after a ship which took part, and with him my mother resumed hunting a few years after the war ended. We hardly ever again, however, had more than two hunters, or one and a pony, and my sisters and I were more often mounted by the kindness of an uncle who lived a few miles away.

When the cob died in about 1920 we bought a second-hand T model Ford of considerable age to bear the brunt of the transport. It was usually open to all weathers but had a hood and talc side-curtains for real downpours. In case of punctures there was a Stepney wheel to be clamped on to the rim to get you home. My mother drove this car and I remember that after cranking it up with a starting handle in front she got it moving by pressing a pedal. A ratchet arrangement on the steering column produced gear changes, the throttle, or accelerator, was a wire with a ring at the end, and a second pedal was the footbrake. It had a klaxon hooter, an appliance which made a screech when you pressed the plunger down, but there was also a bulb horn which sounded more polite and was used for something less than an emergency. This only worked well if you squeezed the rubber bulb slowly and deliberately, a quick grab producing merely a stifled snort.

By this time, however, we had inherited from my grandmother a delightful vehicle called the double dogcart, light-varnished, four-wheeled and with two seats across it; the rear one could be made to face forward or back. The cushions were in a dashing yellow and black check, and indeed it was a very sporting turnout. We used this, by itself or in conjunction with the Ford car, for outings such as picnics and point-to-point races, station work, shopping and fetching the fish, the ice and the laundry. The latter was done every week by the aptly named Mrs Drain, who had washed for my parents when they were at Warley Side and continued to do so until in 1944 a German V2 rocket, landing terrifyingly close, shook her so much that she decided to retire. Prospero had been succeeded by a rather dull brown mare who, almost unprecedentedly for us, never acquired a name, and at the age of about nine to eleven years I was allowed to drive her home, under instruction from the groom, after taking my father to the station in the holidays. Driving a horse still appeared to be a necessary skill, best learnt young, and I have seldom enjoyed anything more or felt more grown-up than when in charge on the box, although nothing could have surpassed the phlegm of the mare and my instructor or the quietness of the road.

It was in the middle 1920s that we became completely mechanized. The Ford was succeeded by an open four-seater Chevrolet with a similar body but controls of a kind which had now become fairly standardized. My brother and I learned to drive on this car, taught by

Murrant in the quieter roads until sent out alone to work out our own salvation and practise reversing. Above all, we learned not to stall the engine for this meant the abominable cranking process. At this time we also had a Sunbeam landaulette, driven only by Murrant; later the Chevrolet was given to my brother at Oxford and replaced at home by a delightful touring Sunbeam which had the luxury of a self-starter. Cars were still idiosyncratic, having ball-changes and gate-changes, some requiring double declutching, with reverse gears of different kinds, controls sometimes on one side and sometimes the other; but we got around with an uneventfulness which said something for our unprofessional and untested tuition.

Learning to drive the car at the age of seventeen was a liberation but there were many competing claims on the cars, and bicycles were essential for everyday purposes. Even my father, who never learned to drive, used to go out to tennis on Sundays on a bicycle, hopping on by a step on the rear hub, to our considerable amusement. Only when an Austin Seven was added for the nominal use of the women of the family, did transport get easier and the embargo on taking the chauffeur out on Sundays cease to blight us. Bikes, however, were still much in use, and a woman's had a certain dignity as it was built much higher than now. It had big wheels with numerous wire spokes and a gear-chain encased in a tin shield to protect one from the oil. From the rear mudguard to the hub a cord dressguard was threaded, to keep long skirts off the wheel. The handlebars were high in relation to the saddle and however low you set them, and however high you raised the saddle, you could never achieve the admired sporting crouch. A good bicycle was beautifully made and repaid the scrupulous cleaning and polishing which a careful owner gave it.

Behind the stable yard and its good brick buildings were the old tarred weatherboarded cowsheds and pigsties. There was a home farm of about a hundred acres and we had four cows, whose names always began with a D like that of their leader, Darkie. They were shorthorns with one Jersey to give richness to the milk. The cowman used to carry the pails to the house with a wooden yoke, shaped to his neck and shoulders. He energetically sluiced down the floors of the old sheds, which must have been very unhygienic nevertheless. The pigsties were extremely smelly and beyond them was a brick-enclosed manure heap in which the stable and farm litter was rotted down for the garden. The woodshed was here too, stacked with logs, and a wet-day job for anyone who had time to spare was to chop some into kindling with the billhook which stood handy on the chopping block. Tools, except the scythe which had its own stone, were sharpened on the circular grinding-stone, moistened from a tin suspended above it. During the 1920s, with the war over and a growing prosperity, the old wooden buildings were demolished and a new brick farmstead built further from the house. Our acquaintance with the cowman, the milking process, the pigfeeding and the cows and calves ceased to be quite so intimate.

Probably owing to the war, and also because ours was a fairly small establishment of its kind, jobs overlapped a good deal. Tom Roscoe, the Lancashire-born head-gardener, also ran the farm in which, from season to season, we saw seedtime and harvest, haymaking, root-picking, harrowing and ploughing, all with horses, Prospero and Matching at first, and after them some heavier carthorses with hairy fetlocks. An old gardener, Fewell, had moved with us from Warley Side; there was an unfit young man, Charlie Sewell, a boy and an elderly cowman until, when the war was over, a more adequate staff of four gardeners worked both the farm and the garden, apart from the cows. Haymaking and harvest saw the whole male workforce simultaneously assembled, sustained by tea and beer sent out from the house. Hot as it often was, the men rarely took off their cloth caps or their waistcoats, and their trousers were of corduroy or thick, stiff, dark cloth, often tied round the knee with a piece of string. The only concession to the weather was the removal of linen or celluloid collars and perhaps the release of the neckband from its brass stud. All the same there was a kind of holiday atmosphere, and we saw the men in a new light, chaffing each other and the temporary helps who turned up, or the maids with the tea, uninhibited by the presence of the nursery or schoolroom party.

Just as the tack room was the nerve-centre of the stables, the potting shed was that of the garden. It was a lean-to of black boarding with a cement floor, up against one of the outside walls of the kitchen garden. As you entered you saw on your right a pit in which stood the coke stove providing heat for the vinery and two other greenhouses, and making the potting shed comfortable on cold days. So comfortable indeed was the place on the wall where the chimney came up that the peacock, named Gabriel Junks out of Surtees' *Handley Cross*, insisted on perching there nearly all the time, instead of displaying on the lawns. What with this, his screeching and his depredations on the garden, he was not replaced when he died a natural death, and the uninteresting peahen was returned to Kelvedon Hall, whence they had both come. The vinery, on which the head-gardener spent a lot of time, stood outside the main walled garden, with a big manured area around it for the roots. The other greenhouses were within the walls and nurtured peaches, nectarines, the succession of pot plants for the porch and conservatory, bulbs and seedlings. On the left of the outer part of the shed was a wooden wheelbarrow; the top half of its container lifted off, according to whether the load to be carried was bulky and light, such as dead leaves, or heavy soil and gravel. Nearby were two boards, about fifteen inches by eight, for scraping up leaves after they had been swept into piles with birch brooms, which stood in a row. Here too were kept large tools not in frequent use; wooden hay rakes, pitchforks, the scythe and, very conspicuous, the four huge leather boots worn by Prospero when he pulled the big mowing-machine once a week. For a day or two afterwards the lawn would have wide regular stripes, demonstrating the great precision with which he was guided and turned. Neither fickle Lady Gay nor our spoilt riding ponies, Pedlar and Peter Pan, would have anything to do with this operation but started playing up as soon as they saw the boots, and would have kicked the machine to pieces.

The inner part of the potting shed was well lit by a window running the length of the high bench used for potting, sowing in boxes and pricking out. The one kitchen chair was seldom sat on, nearly everything being done standing at the bench. There was a cupboard for seeds, fertilizers, small tools, catalogues and string, while a hank of bass hung from the handle. Whole flowerpots of varying sizes were kept under the bench and on one end were the broken ones which provided the crocks put at the bottom of a pot for drainage. A hammer for reducing them to handy sizes lay near and this was a job for wet days. All round the boarded walls were hooks or large nails for tools – sharp-edged spades, the wider shovels, forks, iron rakes, hoes, trowels and sickles. They were kept oiled and rust-free in a beautiful orderliness, the art of which must have been instilled into gardeners for generations, and passed on by them to their juniors. It was rare for new tools to be bought and the handles of the old ones acquired an inimitable satiny finish from years of use. The potting shed régime was very strict but if you properly looked after any tools you used, cleaned and put them back in the right place, never touched the scythe and did jobs at the bench in the approved manner, your presence might be tolerated for long periods. I much preferred these sessions to working in my own patch of garden with the miniature tools provided for our special use.

The strictness of the potting shed extended also to fruit-picking. Nets on tall posts protected the gooseberries, raspberries and black- and red-currants at the far end of the walled garden. These could be eaten freely at any time because most of the gooseberries were picked green for cooking and bottling and those which were left to ripen were not sent into the house for dining-room dessert. Raspberries were so plentiful and went on so long that no restrictions were laid on them, and no one wanted to eat large quantities of raw currants, black or red. Plums and cherries grew on trees trained against the walls and you were allowed to pick any you could reach from the ground. The outdoor peaches and nectarines seldom did well but if there were any we were only allowed windfalls. I have always firmly believed that I once converted a superb peach into a windfall simply by the power of the human eye, which I glued to it one hot afternoon until the fruit dropped with a gentle thud I can hear to this day. Strawberries were grown under low nets which had to be removed for picking, and although we had plenty in the house we were only allowed on the beds at the end of the season when the strawberries were thought to be too small for anything but jam-making. Hothouse grapes, peaches and melons were strictly for grown-up dessert and we only had them as a special treat or if Roscoe picked some out for us from the shallow boxes lined with shavings in which he cherished them for the house till they reached the moment of perfection.

Grapes were treated with particular tenderness so that their bloom should not be rubbed off or the shape of the bunch prematurely spoilt. Fruit was snipped off from the top with special scissors and never, never, must you begin at the bottom or, even worse, pull off a single grape leaving a moist stalk behind. Grown-ups believed then that swallowing so much as one pip would give you that fashionable complaint, appendicitis, so grapes were only eaten under strict supervision until you had mastered the safe and socially acceptable technique. You learned to separate skin and pips with your tongue and eject them neatly into your fingers which you dipped from time to time in your fingerbowl. The clearness or other-wise of the water in it was a good test of your progress in this exacting procedure. Early in the season a bunch of black Hamburghs

Silver grape scissors, 1822

would be sent in, paired with sweet white ones, arranged on a tall-stemmed silver dish so that a few hung temptingly over the side. Later in August the most beautiful of all, the black Madresfield Court with its deep bloom and muscat-flavoured flesh, would appear alone, and last of all the white muscats which tasted better than any and lasted well into September. They usually grew less gracefully than the others and, once a fine bunch had been reserved to hang on the lectern at the Harvest Festival service, several clusters, too flawed for the dining-room, remained to impart to childish palates an inconveniently expensive taste for the best muscatels, raised in hothouses.

The kitchen garden adjoined the Italian garden but was screened from it by a rose-covered trellis in the centre of which an opening led to a broad grass path crossing the vegetable plots. On each side of this was a herbaceous border which was not only one of the best features of the garden but also the source of most of the flowers my mother picked for the house. This border was crossed by another narrower grass path edged with lavender bushes and pink polyanthus roses, and at the intersection was an octagonal trellis for rambler roses. Bedding plants in their season, tulips, wallflowers, geraniums, heliotrope, antirrhinums, dahlias and chrysanthemums bordered a gravel path leading from the back and side doors past the Italian garden to a solid green-painted door in the garden wall, opening on to a lane. Outside there was an all-weather cinder-path, protected from encroaching carts by oak posts about four feet high at about twelve-foot intervals. This was the shortest way to church, half a mile or so away, and we always walked it rather than going by the road, until the diminishing number of coal fires made it impossible any more to find the material for maintaining the path.

Four

THE FRONT HALL

From between ten-foot high hedges of mauve ponticum rhododen-
drons, backed by laurel, the front drive emerged a hundred yards or so
from the side or nursery door, with two tennis courts on the left.
These joined a large area of lawn in front of the house, and at first a
wire fence separated this from the front field. A path between
rosebeds led past the tennis courts to an iron gate into the field. A fine
group of a horse-chestnut, a Scotch fir and a sycamore stood on the
lawn south of the courts and beyond them, as a screen from the road,
was a little wood which we called the front spinney. Various changes
were made in all this during our time. The three trees died one by one
and were not replaced as the light for the courts was better without
them. A thatched summerhouse was built for the comfort of those
watching tennis, the old rosebeds were removed and a new garden
made for them further west, enclosed by yew hedges and a stone
pergola. This linked up with the wooden Japanese bridge put up by
our predecessors, and their charming wild garden full of unusual
plants and old-fashioned roses such as the red and white striped 'York
and Lancaster', moss roses and sweetbriars. A ha-ha was dug the
whole length of the field so that the lawn merged imperceptibly into
the rough grass and trees beyond. The Italian garden and spinney
beyond it, which have already been described, lay on the north side of
the main lawn and west of the house, so we have now made the full
circuit outside.

Between the two bay windows of the central block a white-painted
porch with splayed sides had been built with more of an eye to
comfort than the architectural purity of the front. It was, however, a
considerable amenity as its flat roof made a pleasant place to walk out

31

on from the first-floor room above, and the entrance could be filled with banked-up pot plants, changed according to season. Beside it stood a substantial boot-scraper firmly fixed to the ground, and inside was another one with brushes which, with a coconut mat, ensured that little mud would be brought into the house. Nevertheless the red-tiled floor was scrubbed often so that the porch, into which the sun streamed through ample windows, had something of the fragrant humidity of a hothouse. The oak inner front door was never locked except at night and you pushed it open and walked through into the oak-panelled hall which at first seemed dark after the sunny porch. To the right was first an oak table which I think was Georgian, very plain with straight tapered legs and an inset band of darker wood, perhaps mahogany, round its edge. It had two shallow drawers in which were kept rulers, the tape measure in a leather case for marking out the tennis courts, a hammer and a few other simple tools. On it stood an oak letter box about a foot high with a brass slot. In theory you 'posted' letters in it but they were apt to be overlooked if you did, so usually they were placed on top for the butler to collect, stamp and take or send to the post at about 5 pm. Incoming letters were put on the table and it was the rule of the house that we never normally commented on what had arrived and from whom. The exception was postcards which were the means of communicating trains to be met and other such arrangements requiring liaison. Notes brought by hand and the visiting cards of callers were left here too, and there was also the red leather frame with IN on one side and OUT on the other. This was turned round appropriately according to whether my mother was in and available to visitors, or not wanting to be seen, or well and truly out of the house. The doorbell rang near the pantry and unless it went on ringing unanswered we never opened the front door ourselves. This would be done by the butler or footman who would take a note or card straight into his hand but put it on a salver to give to my father or mother. The idea behind this, pejoratively described as 'feudal' by my father but nevertheless adhered to, was that the employee's hand was somehow different from a hand of employer status.

Paying social calls had its own elaborate ritual. Older residents called on newcomers after they had met them somewhere or somehow received a reasonably favourable report or impression when they established themselves within the radius of about eight miles, which was the limit for horses. The recipient of the call then returned it and the original caller would invite the other to luncheon, dinner, a tennis party, or some more generalized entertainment such as a dance, after which normal social intercourse set in. It did not matter if the callers found each other in or not; in either case they left visiting cards engraved in copperplate with their name and address. My mother's card was about three by two inches, and her daughters' names were added to it when they grew up. I think she left one of hers and two of my father's smaller card on a married couple, one of his and one of hers on a widow, but only her own on a spinster. He would leave his alone on bachelors such as the officers at the Guards' and Essex Regiment's messes at Warley Barracks. When we first arrived at Pilgrims' Hall my mother had a lot of calls to return and often took me with her, perhaps to relieve what I now recognize was her acute shyness. Usually rather queasy from the brougham and always warily silent with strangers, I cannot have helped very much. We would be dressed in our best clothes, driven by the coachman as she never took the reins herself on these occasions, and we would both earnestly hope that the people would be out which, luckily for themselves and us, they often were. After a time, of course, we became the old hands who paid the first call, and she then deformalized the procedure and took a short cut to the invitation stage. However, there still seemed to be a lot of visiting cards lying about, and they were kept for years in a Chinese bowl in the hall, for reference as to initials and addresses.

Continuing round the hall, we come to one of the long low leaded windows which were out of period and must have been put in when the room was oak-panelled in a fortunately restrained neo-Jacobean style. In the window recess stood a high-backed Queen Anne chair and at the corner was the door to the dining-room. There was a thick wall here which must have been an outside one before the addition of the wings, and two rather treacherous steps down were for adjustment to a fall in the ground. To the left was a walnut-framed looking-glass, handy for the ladies who might want to resettle their hats before going in to the meal. Everyone not living or staying in the house wore hats at luncheon and even my mother kept hers on after having been out, or even deliberately put one on. Putting-on is the right expression because grand hats were perched on top of the hair-do and secured by often very elaborate and always rather dangerous hatpins. You only crammed your head into hats intended for bad weather. Further along was a Queen Anne walnut chest of drawers on a stand, faded to a dull gold. The top lefthand drawer held my father's gloves, and the righthand one the prayerbooks to take to church on Sundays, and a clothes brush. The first long drawer held some favourite toys and books, including among the latter, one with strings which, when pulled, made farmyard noises to match the pictures, and two volumes of biblical animals, deliciously terrifying because the scorpion was the same size as the lion. The next drawer contained brown paper for wrapping up parcels and the third, deepest, one records for the pianola. A shallow one in the stand was a repository for maps and large unframed photographs which had not quite won through to being put on display.

Next came the five steps of the lower flight of stairs, from which turned the upper flight of thirteen. The house was rather dark here, with switches inconveniently placed, and one counted the steps for safety. They were broad and shallow, covered with thick chocolate-brown pile carpet, held in place by bright steel rods, square in section, leaving a few inches of polished oak visible at the end of each tread. The stairs led to the main upper landing, similarly carpeted, and from here, by looking over or through an oak balustrade, chidren and dogs could assess the situation below before descending. At the angle of the stairs, partly hiding an invaluable glory-hole, was a large walnut Steck piano with pianola player incorporated. We were a very unmusical family and soon piano lessons were given up as hopeless, but everybody enjoyed playing the pianola and it was used for grown-ups to dance to and for children's Musical Chairs. This very favourite game involved circling a row of chairs, always one short, so that the player who failed to get one when the music stopped was out, and so on round by round until the chairs were reduced to one, and the players, down to two finalists, jumpily circling it until the winner managed to sit down on the last note. When I was in my teens the pianola was largely superseded by a gramophone, an His Master's Voice table model in an oak box.

The inside of the piano, which we saw exposed when the tuner, Winter, came about every three months, was a mass of air-pipes as well as the ordinary wires and hammers. To play a record you slid back a panel above the keyboard, inserted one of the punched paper rolls, attached the string on the end of it to a lower roller, and then pounded away at the big pedals which opened out from a recess in the base. A flap under the keyboard dropped down to show a row of brass controls for starting, rewinding, or altering speed and volume. At the end you reeled back until the string which had secured the roll released itself and rattled sharply round. You then took out the roller, tightened it by turning one end, which made a characteristic squeak, twisted the string round a button and put the record back into its long cardboard box in its own place in the drawer. There were about twenty of them; I remember selections from Gilbert and Sullivan and from Elgar, 'The Blue Danube', the 'Moonlight' sonata, some foxtrots and marches.

Under the stairs, hidden by a painted leather screen of oriental design, were kept the spare leaves for the dining-room table, a beautifully made camphorwood chest for furs, and the round 'Eaton' tea table. Its two semi-circular leaves folded flat against each other, on crossed legs, for storage – a very handy design, seen in many houses and often given as a wedding present.

We nearly always had tea in the hall, at the fireplace end. It would be brought in at 4.30 pm either by the butler or footman, who took it in turns to be on duty and answer the door in the afternoons. The fashion in tablecloths changed from plain white to a shade called écru, both lightly embroidered, then to coarser linen with coloured stripes. In winter an Art Nouveau covered dish with a blister-pearl finial was put near the fire on a brass tripod and this contained hot scones, buns, crumpets, hot buttered toast or anchovy toast. A wooden cakestand, its three circular tiers folding flat on a rod when put away, held plates of usually rather plain cakes and biscuits. On the table would be a plate of thin cut bread and butter, a pot of jam from the Tiptree factory, and perhaps sandwiches. For many years the tea service was white with a green and gilt leaf border, of a design which can still be bought from Goode's china shop. It was followed by a fine Rockingham, a silver-wedding present, in dark pink, white and gold in a chequer pattern, but the breakages in this too-fragile set became tragic and it was replaced by a sturdier yellow-banded modern Wedgwood.

An oval mahogany tray with a shell centre in marquetry, and brass handles, was set in front of my mother's place and on this were a reproduction early Georgian silver teapot, an Irish silver sugar bowl and milk-jug on little legs, the china slop bowl belonging to the tea-set,

Plated muffin dish, *c.* 1906

and the cups and saucers, ready for filling and distributing. Hot water was provided by a big silver tea-kettle, a Victorian copy of an eighteenth-century design but so long used and polished that it had acquired the delicacy of an antique. It was fixed by two pins to a tripod stand holding a methylated spirit lamp, the front pin forming a hinge while the back one anchored the kettle to the stand for carrying. All went well unless someone forgot to pull out the rear pin before pouring, for then the jolt and tipping of the stand spilled out heated methylated spirit which would take fire from the lighted wick, and the whole contraption would burst into flames. It was, however, always stood on a separate galler-ied silver tray, which to some extent contained the disaster until the kettle could be removed to the

Tea-kettle

fender. Most people had similar kettles but I never saw anyone else's behave like this and I think visitors must sometimes have been surprised at my mother's nonchalant coping with the situation. Another fascinating feature of the kettle routine was that a tapering silver tube about ten inches long, with flat mouthpiece, was always laid on the tray; you could extinguish the flame by inserting this in the pierced guard of the lamp and blowing sharply. Such implements, called douters, I have since discovered, were a late-Victorian refinement, cutting out inelegant puffing.

In the long north wall of the hall were doors leading to the service quarters and to the rooms in the west wing. Between them was a big oak chest, almost black, in which were kept tennis rackets with their presses, hockey sticks for the mixed matches played in the neighbour-hood on winter Sunday afternoons, a seldom-used cricket bat and several boxes of delicious-smelling Slazenger tennis balls. To clean them there was a wooden cylindrical appliance with brushes inside, but we took our tennis seriously and were prodigal with new balls. In the west wall was a big open fireplace for a log fire, with a leather-covered settle round it. My mother wrote at a fine antique walnut bureau shielded from draughts, at least in theory, by another oriental screen. In fact there were very few places in the house which were free from draughts as the passages were very cold and probably their chill was drawn into the rooms by the fires. A somewhat rudimentary central heating system which we inherited was abandoned during the 1914 war and it was not until the late 1920s that it was got going again, never very satisfactorily. Like most other children we knew, we were martyrs to chilblains and colds in the head, and the nursery often reeked with camphorated oil and eucalyptus, the specific remedies used for these complaints. However, cold or not, my mother used to sit for hours at her bureau writing family letters, which she did extremely well, dealing with the household orders and bills, references and 'characters' which went with the employment of a large domestic staff, and the paperwork for the Soldiers' and Sailors' Help Society, the District Nursing Association and the Mothers' Union, her principal concerns among many parish activities. I used to be paid threepence a dozen to docket the household receipts, which were kept for seven years; I picked up much curious information about water rates and tithes, upholstery and turnery, china replacement and the tinning of copper saucepans, and the mysterious licences for Armorial Bearings, Male Servants and Dogs. The day-to-day tradesmen's accounts were entered by hand in leather-covered books, brought for settlement once a month, and the butcher's had a handsome ox outlined in gilt on its red cover.

The big log fire was nearly the means of burning the house down when I was about nine. The tarry deposit in the chimney defied the sweep's routine attentions and caught fire one day so that old beams got involved and smoke was found to be issuing from crevices in the rooms upstairs. We children did not know anything was amiss until the fire engine arrived at the gallop in the front drive. It was a wonderful affair, all scarlet paint and brass, drawn by four horses who stood and steamed in the sleety cold until my mother sent us to fetch rugs for them from the harness room. The firemen made a tremendous mess with their hoses and from hacking away at wainscots with their axes, but they soon put the fire out, leaving a long-lasting nauseous smell of damp charred wood. They had dark blue uniforms, high boots and beautiful brass helmets with a grand badge on the front. They were led by Sergeant Smith, whose huge yellow-grey moustache curled over and around his brass chinstrap; he and his men stayed for some time chatting round the devastated fireplace, probably waiting to see if the fire broke out again.

There followed what must have been a very uncomfortable winter in the front part of the house and this was one of the few occasions I can remember when much internal decoration was done. Outside painting was normally carried out every three years, the porch and window-frames in white, the ironwork in black, the doors of house, stable, garage and garden in green. Yet in the more than fifty years we had the house the drawing-room was only painted twice. The dining-room had its walls changed from white to eggshell green when a new chimneypiece was put in, but not again. The best spare-room was redecorated once, its white paint being changed to pale green, and the other bedrooms no oftener. My father's smoking-room, its shelves almost entirely lined with books, was never repainted; nor was the billiard-room, but the area of paint above the panelling in the hall was once refreshed. The kitchen and other back premises were done very thoroughly on one occasion, as were the nurseries when they later became our bedrooms. The paint must have been of first-rate quality to withstand the strenuous spring-cleaning of many years, but around the brilliantly polished brass doorknobs and bolts there was generally an area of plain wood produced by the friction.

On the opposite side of the hall fireplace from my mother's bureau was the door to the drawing-room; then a long window matched the one at the other side of the front entrance, where we started our tour of the room. A high-backed Queen Anne chair and an oak coffin-stool stood in the window recess, while beyond it was a walnut table with cabriole legs. On this lay *The Times*, *The Times Literary Supplement*, and *The Morning Post*; two local weeklies; *Punch*, *The Sphere* or *The Illustrated London News*, *Country Life*, and *The Connoisseur*; at different periods we took *The Spectator*, *The Nation*, *The Weekend Review* or *The New Statesman*. My father always bought an evening paper to read in the train and this was taken up to the governess with her supper. It was, I think, the greenish *Westminster Gazette*. The illustrated weeklies were eagerly awaited, and patient grown-ups would explain the *Punch* jokes and, to the best of their ability, the cartoons, some of which have passed into history. We were familiar enough with Britannia and John Bull, Uncle Sam, Big and Little Willie, the King of the Belgians, Asquith and Lloyd George; nor could you fault us on the flags of the Allies. A long sofa, loose-covered in blue linen or floral cretonne, bisected the hall, and there were two big armchairs to match. On a table to the right of the sofa was the china bowl which held old visiting cards, with ashtrays, matches, cigarettes and a rack of green gilt-stamped covers holding the *ABC* and *Bradshaw* railway time-tables, *Whitaker's Almanack* and the *Postal Guide*. New ones were supposed to be put in the covers each year but in practice only the timetables were ever renewed, and of these the latest were put near the telephone. Here also lay the green leatherbound Visitors' Book, in which people who had been staying would write their names, addresses and the dates of their visit before they departed.

The wall-panelling ended about two feet from the ceiling with a ledge on which were ranged about a hundred Famille Rose plates of floral design. These represented my father's share of his mother's dinner service which had been in everyday use for a large family for many years. Their brilliant hard paste had stood up remarkably well to being washed in soda or made red-hot in the oven, but he recognized their quality and removed them from such tests. For many years there were no pictures in the hall but as my parents bought or inherited them, some landscape water-colours were hung there: a de Wint, a David Cox, two Thorne Waites, two Harringtons, a Bertram Nicholls and a Gerald Ackermann. There was always a big vase of flowers on the walnut chest, a pot plant or bowl of flowers on the table with the book rack, and a small vase on the chimneypiece. The cult of flower decoration had not spread much then, and different kinds were not usually mixed. To me, the tall glass or earthenware vases of lupins, peonies or chrysanthemums, the bowls of roses or forget-me-nots, the slim trumpet-shaped glasses of sweet peas, seem infinitely more attractive.

It was perhaps a sombre room, with its oak-panelling, heavy dark gold curtains, deep red and purplish Persian rugs, and the bronzes on the chimneypiece. There was brightness, however, in the Chinese plates, the English red lacquer clock and the gleaming silver sconces over the fireplace. It was the very heart of the house, full of the talk and activity of the life we lived so much in common – parents, children, visitors, staff, and always one very spoilt dog determined not to be left out of anything.

Five

THE DINING-ROOM

The dining-room was probably ahead of its time in having plain white-painted walls, but an elaborate reddish mahogany chimney piece made up from a four-poster bed remained from our predecessors' much darker colour scheme. It was subsequently replaced by a good carved Georgian one and the walls painted pale green. The builder who put in the fireplace pulled a long face when he found it was not only secondhand but obviously very old, and he broke it gently to my father that he thought he had been done. The ceiling had a bold design of fruit and flowers in high-relief papier-mâché and from the centre of each large roundel of its main motif hung a beautiful veined brown and white translucent alabaster bowl mounted in gilt bronze. The light from electric bulbs inside was reflected softly and slightly rosily from the white ceiling. The ground colour of the carpet was pink, and the effect much more sympathetic than might have been expected from this product of Turkey, so hardwearing that it is still in use after more than sixty years.

On the right as you entered from the hall was a bow-window in which stood a reproduction Chippendale settee with a brocade seat. On each side of it were big Chinese jars covered with deer and little fir trees in brown and green on a white ground. Next came a delicate Georgian sideboard of varied mahogany veneers, with a cellarette standing underneath. The latter contained liqueurs but, except for cherry brandy in the Christmas season, these were seldom brought out, port being the usual ending to dinner. On the sideboard, on a white drawn-thread work table runner, stood dishes of fruit, and dessert plates. Each of these had its silver knife and fork, and a glass fingerbowl standing on a doily, a little mat of lace or very fine linen

Side-table in dining-room

which prevented the bowl sliding about on the plate or depositing a drip when removed on to the table. We had two dessert services, a contemporary Minton of the Cockatrice design in green for every day, and a very treacherous Dresden with pierced edges to the plates, used only for parties. A high wide french window led into the conservatory, which had a red-tiled floor and tiered stands for plants. Like those in the front porch these were changed according to season and sometimes offered a wonderful display. Here too was the lemon verbena whose fragrant narrow leaves were floated in the fingerbowls, and a 'sensitive plant' which we used to tease in idle moments. The curtains were of dark green velvet.

The rather dim corner next to the window was furnished with spare chairs ranged against the walls, and in the north wall came the big fireplace with steel basket grate in which, in winter, there was always a huge coal fire, banked down with coal-dust, or slack as they called it, between meals. The fire-screen beside it had often to be put in position for the benefit of the person whose back was to the fire. Coal was kept in a bright steel scuttle and the substantial poker, tongs and shovel were of bright steel as well. Next came the butler's tray on trestles, where dishes were deposited before being brought out from behind the tall six-leaved stamped-leather screen which hid the red baize service-door to the back premises. The smell of cooking was anathema and this door was kept shut as much as possible.

The serving table on which the carving was done or the breakfast dishes set out was a reddish Victorian mahogany affair with bulbous legs and a silk curtain on a brass rail to prevent splashing of the wall. It looked rather like a sturdy pony beside a thoroughbred, standing as it did next to the fine Chippendale serpentine-fronted side-table which occupied most of the remaining space up to the main door. On this stood the silver Duke of Wellington and his charger Copenhagen, presented to my grandfather as first Clerk to the Governors of Wellington College. This was a popular statuette which I have seen elsewhere and probably the sculptor was one of the Garrards whose name is that of the firm which made it. Two tall silver candlesticks, adapted for electricity, stood beside him and the rest of the space was devoted to decanters, spare glasses and cutlery: straightsided and square decanters for spirits, less heavily cut ones for port and sherry, with rounded sides and longer necks. Enamelled labels on little chains indicated their contents. In the early days whisky noggins were placed beside my father and male guests at lunchtime, but the custom of drinking whisky and soda with lunch must have died out and these charming little objects were relegated to a cupboard. They were plain glass flasks with handles, containing perhaps a quarter-pint; their flat silver lids opened with a thumb-piece and round the necks were small silver labels engraved with the word Whiskey, spelt in the Irish manner. The soda-water syphons which accompanied them came from Schweppes and were returned periodically to the makers for refilling.

The dining table was round, of french-polished dark mahogany, about six feet in diameter. It could be wound apart by means of a brass handle for extra leaves to be inserted for parties, but without such additions it easily seated six. It was a modern one, made for my parents, and the polish was very delicate, developing an irremovable greyish bloom if something too hot were put on

Silver candlestick, 1895, converted for electricity

it. In the daytime it was usually covered with thick felt and a white tablecloth, the bare polish only being exposed in the evening at dinner, with heatproof place-mats under linen squares in drawn-thread work. In the centre would be a trumpet-shaped glass vase of flowers, a silver rose bowl or one of several ornamental cups. The chairs were of a shieldback Hepplewhite design, copied from one pair of genuine old ones which had pieces of stamp paper stuck on their undersides to remind us to spare them undue wear and tear. The reproductions were so good as to be virtually indistinguishable and they illustrated the robust attitude to antiques shown by many people of my parents' generation. If they liked an old design, whether of furniture or silver, they had it copied to make up a set by the excellent craftsmen working at the time, and without any intention to deceive. No old design was tolerated merely for historical reasons. If it were uncomfortable or too large or too fragile it failed to earn a place: thus the antiques and the reproductions, or frankly modern oak, walnut and mahogany; the eighteenth-, nineteenth- or twentieth-century silver, Sheffield or electro plate, jogged along in a harmony engendered by long use and wear. One pear-shaped silver jug which, at our ultimate sale, turned out to be Louis Quinze and quite rare, was always highly unpopular. Its lid was difficult to hold up for pouring anything hot and, rather masochistically, we only used it for cocoa after chilly evening meetings in the draughty school or the village club. We let it go without a pang.

On the right of the door from the hall was a crayon by Richmond of my greatgrandfather Bacon in his younger days and, on the other side of the window, the seascape by Somerscales I remembered from my former home. Later this was moved and replaced by a portrait of my mother's uncle, the Master of Foxhounds, on horseback at the covertside with a few hounds. A good deal later there arrived my father's excellent portrait by George Harcourt, a Wilson Steer landscape and a painting of the house by Rex Whistler. The latter came in June 1936 and sat all one grey and icy day making a very detailed pencil drawing from which he did the oil painting in his studio without coming to the house again. He was charming and enthusiastic but so pale that we guiltily wondered if he had caught his death of cold and it was only after some months that we began to feel that delivery was unduly slow. He placated my father, who was getting cross, by a gift of seats for the dress rehearsal of *Victoria Regina*, for which he had designed the décor, and not too long after that the picture arrived to delight us all. Though it is accurate enough he painted not so much a matured landscape as a divination of the original vision which had inspired its designers. On his canvas the dream came true with house and garden just a little more perfectly composed than in real life and bathed in evening sunshine such as I am afraid he never saw.

On the other side of the conservatory door were a rather dull Farquharson of sheep and cornstooks, a not very good Dutch landscape and a Callcot, 'The Phantom Ship', which was a favourite. Over the chimneypiece was a dark picture, 'Spanish Dancers', by Jacomb Hood, replaced afterwards by Holl's portrait of my great-grandfather in old age, inherited from a cousin. Beyond, half-hidden by a screen, was the portrait of a pretty kinswoman, irremediably ruined by some Victorian great-aunts who had prudishly had a too-dashing *décolletage* painted out in dark bituminous draperies. Above the serving table hung a little heathery landscape by Leader and a delightful oil sketch of a woman's head by Inskipp. Over the centre of the big side-table was a beautiful Chinese Chippendale gilt mirror, flanked by my Lawrence grandfather's portrait by Holl and my grandmother's by Tuke, in sombre Victorian black. And that brings us back to where we started round the room.

Our first introduction to dining-room meals was Sunday luncheon, then we were promoted to everyday luncheon and breakfast, and finally, in our teens, to the full panoply of dinner in the evening which, till then, we had only seen on Christmas Day. Breakfast was ready punctually at 8 am Mondays to Fridays, 8.30 on Saturdays and 8.45 on Sundays. We could come down a little late at weekends without exciting comment but only guests were privileged, indeed encouraged, to appear some minutes after the gong on weekdays. As in nearly all the other households I knew, the meal was almost completely silent, except for my parents commenting perhaps on a letter or on something in the newspaper propped up in front of my father. In the middle of the table was the Georgian mahogany 'dumb waiter', a circular tray with scalloped edge revolving on three claw feet and loaded

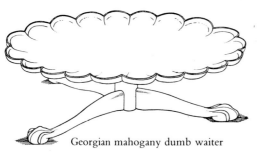

Georgian mahogany dumb waiter

with toast, butter, marmalade and sugar which could thus be passed round in silence. During the short period of rationing at the end of the 1914–18 war our individual pats of butter and sugar bowls were set out on it, and a certain amount of conversation tended to develop when supplies ran low at the end of the week and barter set in. I think now that the extreme irascibility of even normally genial men at breakfast was due to port, which disagreed with them without their knowing it. Lovingly they cradled priceless cobwebby bottles up the cellar steps and, so as not to disturb the sediment, broke the necks off clean by means of special tongs, made red-hot in the pantry fire, and the subsequent application of a cold wet cloth. Hardly breathing, they would pour it through a silver strainer into a glass decanter which would then be left on the dining-room chimneypiece with the stopper out, to take on the temperature of the room. Then they would gently poison themselves with a modest one glass a night, perhaps two or three at a party, and come down to breakfast like bears with sore heads. Unduly bright young men staying in the house risked never being invited again if they made facetious remarks before, to everyone's relief, the host had left the table.

Breakfast was delicious nevertheless. On weekdays there were two heavy Victorian plated dishes with hot water bases on the serving table. In these would be variations on eggs and bacon, kippers, dried haddock, fishcakes, kedgeree or kidneys. On Saturdays and Sundays the electric heater was used, with lighter oval entrée dishes of which the lids could also be used as dishes when their detachable handles were removed. In the winter on Sundays there were sausages and instead of a second dish we could boil our own eggs in a plated egg-shaped container, measuring into the lamp underneath it just the right amount of methylated spirit for the job. The contents of the breakfast dishes were accurately estimated and we were expected to finish them up. At other meals, when the dishes were handed, we were supposed to leave a little for 'Mr Manners' to show that enough had been sent in – a mistake, we felt, when perhaps it had not. The silver tea-kettle stood in front of my mother and she made Indian tea for herself and us in the same teapot we used at teatime. My father had China tea in his own bullet-shaped pot, the amount being measured with

Plated egg-boiler, c. 1906

the top of his cylindrical caddy. The staff had breakfast in the servants' hall at the same time as we did and waiting on parents and visitors in the dining-room was done by the children.

My companion for lessons, Clemency Chamen, arrived at 9.15 and we then started work with the governess, having previously fed the rabbits. At 10 my mother went into the kitchen to confer with the cook about the day's meals or, if it was Friday, those for the weekend. In early days the list was written on a slate with a slate pencil which, to my ears, squeaked deliciously when I was allowed to use it. I envied the schoolchildren who used slates habitually and indeed admired them altogether for their supposedly greater freedom and knowledge of the world. They used to troop past the drive gates in a spasmodic progress punctuated by bouts of the current game. It was either skipping, conkers, marbles, hoops, whipping-tops or hopscotch, which followed some mysterious cycle. We had hoops too but we were only allowed wooden ones driven with a nicely turned stick instead of the much more exciting iron ones which ran through a hook, making a noise which children loved and grown-ups abominated. It was not until I joined the Girl Guides that I discovered the restrictions under which my village colleagues also suffered, and found them little more sophisticated than I.

After our slate got broken the cook used an exercise book instead, and a pile of old ones in the corner of a kitchen shelf provided mouth-watering reading during the 1939–45 war. It seemed incredible how much we had eaten but what with keeping out the cold and expending so much energy in getting from one place to another I suppose we could burn it all up and still stay thin. Fat adults were not uncommon but fat children were rare enough to be regarded as freaks, poor things.

To return, however, to the dining-room, for luncheon. My father would normally only be there on Saturdays and Sundays and the usual weekday party was my mother, the governess and two or three children. Visitors had to put up with silent poker-faced witnesses, supposed to be seen and not heard and not to speak unless spoken to, but who missed absolutely nothing. Some would feel constrained to bring the children into the conversation but this was not usually a success and we preferred to be ignored. We had our own troubles because we were under the eye of the butler and footman and this took some getting used to after the relaxed atmosphere of the nursery. Nanny was not strict at all, despite her unsmiling expression, and with her we were terribly finicky and outspoken about food to which we took dislikes. Occasionally perhaps she sympathized with us for there was a slight chronic feud between kitchen and nursery, and if her one glass of beer was flat she was not at all amused. Generally it effervesced gaily and when I first heard the line 'beaded bubbles winking at the brim' it seemed perfectly to describe Nanny's brimming tumbler. If she was displeased about anything like this it was conveyed only by atmosphere or meaning glances at the nurserymaid because interdepartmental solidarity was rigorously maintained in front of us.

In the dining-room carving was done by the butler at the serving table, plates set before us by the footman, and vegetables and sauces handed by both of them from the left side. Vegetables came in a big round plated dish with a triple partition and a draining plate at the bottom; sauces in silver sauceboats of Georgian pattern; gravy in a Sheffield plate 'Argyll', an urn-shaped vessel with a wooden heat-insulated handle, a curved spout at right-angles and an outer skin for hot water, filled through a lip opposite the gravy spout. Except for the vegetable dish, which had its own handle, everything was brought to one's elbow on a silver salver which one had to try very hard not to drop drips on. We were exhorted not to 'mug' the silver, a heinous offence, and learned to pick up objects quickly and cleanly, leaving as few fingermarks as possible on plain surfaces, and never breathing over or into the christening-cups from which we drank. Indeed breathing was very much discouraged in the dining-room. When we were small the table silver was of the heavy Victorian 'King's Pattern', which did not show marks much and did not bend. As we grew more civilized, however, my parents reverted to the much worn plain Georgian set which they always preferred. We must not ask for anything but must wait to be offered it, must take the nearest instead of choosing the best, and leave nothing but obviously inedible remains on our plates. Rescue, however, always came when the course was cleared away as a matter of routine, and I think the staff were on our side in this.

On the whole the menservants were reliable, did not tell tales and treated us with healthy detachment. One footman was, however, a terrible tease and our great aim was to keep from him anything he might castigate as childish. Contrary to custom he was local and had been promoted from the rank of houseboy, hence his name Tommy, so far from the dignified Charles, Henry or Frederick to which the others answered. Having grown up with us he knew far too much about us, our games and particularly the parts we were playing. My schoolroom mate Clemency and I lived most of our waking lives as characters in a country of our invention called Palmland. We drew maps of it and, with pencils and watercolour, endlessly illustrated the exploits of its inhabitants and its enemies, the Blackfeet, whom we always soundly defeated in battle. Usually we impersonated the commanders-in-chief, Sir Edward Fitzgerald and Sir Alfred Robey, but we might switch to others and we did not like Tommy getting hold of their names and hissing them in our ears in a mocking way. We used to implore the governess not to tell Tommy any 'secrets', something which she indignantly and justifiably protested she would never think of doing. There was leakage but it must have been through younger sisters.

Luncheon started with the main dish and it was only towards the end of the period I am remembering that a starter course was served, even with guests. On Sundays there was hot roast beef and Yorkshire pudding, occasionally varied by chicken or mutton. These provided cold meat for Mondays, often with potatoes baked in their jackets, and might stretch to cottage pie, rissoles or hashed mutton on Tuesdays. Otherwise we might have liver and bacon or, only too rarely, sausage and mash, sausages on the whole being reserved for Sunday breakfast. Wednesday lunch would be another joint, almost invariably mutton, either roast, with onion or mint sauce, or boiled with caper sauce, a dish appreciated by grown-ups but abhorred by all right-thinking children. On Thursdays the remains would be made up in some way and on Fridays we usually had fish. This was not for religious reasons but because, for some consideration probably involved with transport, it fitted in. On Saturdays in winter there would be beefsteak pie or pudding, Lancashire hotpot, Irish stew, boiled beef with dumplings and, in summer, cold meat with salad dressed by my father on the sideboard. Sunday pudding was usually a huge apple, gooseberry or other fruit tart with cream or custard. On other days changes were rung on stewed fruit with rice, sago or semolina milk puddings, steamed chocolate, ginger or lemon sponges with appropriate sauces, suet rolls with jam, currants or treacle, baked apples and apple dumplings. At weekends, or whenever we had visitors, the pudding was followed by cheese, biscuits and butter in a triple-compartmented china dish. Wine did not very often appear at luncheon and the women usually drank water or home-made lemonade, and the men beer. Coffee was handed in the dining-room when we were alone, but for parties and at weekends was taken into the hall or drawing-room. A silver tray was laid with little green and gold cups, miniature apostle spoons and two pots which matched each other although they were not a pair, one being of old silver and one of Sheffield plate, both with spiral fluting. Luncheon was ready punctually at 1 pm and as regarded any waiting to be done was virtually finished by 1.30, when the staff had theirs. The butler or footman emerged at about 2.45 to see visitors out.

One ceremony was never omitted and this was the supervision of the dog's dinner. When there were visitors the plate was just shown to my mother before being put down for the dog, who had been lying under the table among the hassocks thoughtfully provided for people with short legs. If we were alone she would add titbits to the basic biscuits and gravy to make it look appetizing. There was a cautionary tale about doing this while talking to guests as my mother's family had once seen an absent-minded hostess eat the whole of her dog's dinner before their eyes. They never forgot that.

Unless there was a big tea for a children's party or tennis the dining-room was not entered again until preparations for dinner began. This meal was at 7.45 when we were alone, 8 o'clock for a party. We almost invariably dressed for it, the men in dinner-jackets or velvet smoking-jackets, over stiff-fronted shirts with wing collars and black bow ties until at some time in the 1930s soft evening shirts became permissible. Women doggedly wore out their old party dresses, covering up the unwelcome exposure of shoulders and arms with a variety of shawls, fur stoles and bright little jackets, very, very necessary if you were sitting on the far side away from the fire. For a party, usually of eight, the wrappings would be shed and the men would put on white ties and black tailcoats, except for the hunting men who in winter wore scarlet ones with the gilt buttons of their Hunt Club. Elaborately as we were dressed we could achieve it in a very short time, helped by the maids, who dropped things over our heads, did us up at the back and cleared up the chaos we had left after changing from that last set too many of tennis. My mother started in good time but tended to get side-tracked, and if we were assembled in the drawing-room the chandelier would bounce and tinkle from all the activity just above it. A faint whiff of singeing hair would invade the house while she curled the fringe on her forehead with the little methylated spirit lamp out of her dressing case. Unlike her daughters, she did not want help in dressing but guests arriving early must have thought from the vibrating chandelier that their composed and perfectly groomed hostess had been the centre of a whole team of frenzied assistants.

Dinner always started with soup, ladled by the butler into red-hot plates from the serving table, and handed round by the footman. Then there was fish of the less substantial kind – fillets of sole or haddock, whiting curled with the tail through the head, whitebait or scallops. The meat course was usually something to be handed round rather than carved – cutlets in various guises, steaks or casseroles; but grouse, partridges and pheasants, in their short seasons, always appeared at dinner rather than luncheon and were carved by the butler. The grouse would be presents from Scotland, arriving expeditiously by post in cardboard boxes lined with heather. The pheasants and partridges came from my father's shoot or from the friends he shot with. When alone we would have a sweet course or a savoury such as Scotch Woodcock, which was scrambled egg on anchovy toast, Angels on Horseback, which were chicken liver or an oyster wrapped in bacon, toasted cheese or a cheese soufflé, or sardines on toast. The menu was always written on a white china slate, in a mixture of English and the cook's plucky efforts at French, and if there was both sweet and savoury you usually chose either one or the other. The puddings were lighter than at luncheon and we would have custards baked or boiled, fruit fools, lemon cheese or jam tartlets, pancakes, fritters and never the plain milk puddings which only my mother really liked.

For a party of eight or more the menu was written on cards stuck into two pairs of holders, the enamelled Balliol crest ones and the silver foxes. A name card was put at each place, my father sitting with his back to the fire, the principal lady on his right and the next in precedence on his left. If there was a bride she would always be put on his right, regardless of age or anything else. The senior men sat on each side of my mother at the other end of the table, leaving a bit of a rabble in the middle where the younger members of the family did their entertaining. The polished table was laid with an ornamental cup in the centre, or a large vase of flowers with smaller ones round it. At intervals there would be silver salts, peppers and mustard pots and little dishes of salted almonds. Each place would be laid with the full complement of cutlery: a tablespoon for soup, fish knife and fork, meat knife and fork, dessert spoon and fork and cheese knife and fork for the savoury, with a sherry glass, wine glass and tumbler for everyone. A white table napkin, folded to stand upright, marked each place and at no meal were these ever re-used. Napkin rings were unknown to us. After the savoury the table was cleared of everything except the central ornaments and the top lights were switched off, leaving only the wall sconces and candelabra. Fruit plates with fingerbowls and dessert cutlery were put down instead of the place-mats which had been removed, port glasses were set out, my father sent the decanter round and the servants left the room. After a short interval to allow the women to drink a glass of port if they wanted to my mother would lead them out to powder their noses in her bedroom and drink coffee in the drawing-room. What the men did then of course I never saw but I think they shifted their chairs closer together near the fire before having some more port and perhaps some brandy and cigars. The guests might start to leave at any time after 10.30 and it was unusual for the party to go on till midnight.

Far from being inhibiting this elaborate ritual promoted a convivial atmosphere and good talk. There were no interruptions for service because under a good butler plate succeeded plate as if by magic, the monogram on the gold and white key pattern china always being placed precisely at the top. Everything was handed in its correct order and all noises off, of which there must have been many, were quickly shut away behind the baize door. However good the food, and indeed it was very good, it was seldom commented on although the men discussed the wines and were probably expected to. The presence of the domestic staff seemed not to limit the freedom of conversation but I realize now that this freedom must have been relative and that considerable reticence was so engrained as to be habitual. I was never aware of anyone having too much to drink although my father was the most generous of hosts and the wine flowed.

DRAWING-ROOM, SMOKING-ROOM AND BILLIARD-ROOM

The hall was the mildly Jacobean fantasy of some predecessor and dated perhaps from about the 1890s; but when you passed through the oak-panelled door on the left of the fireplace the style became the neo-Georgian of the Edwardian period which was the keynote of the house. There was first a white-panelled passage or lobby about three feet long corresponding to the thickness of the original outside wall, as was the case with the dining-room. Here, however, there was a second, inner door, which was usually kept open with a long-handled brass doorstop weighted by a lion at the foot. The drawing-room itself was a big light room with a bow-window to the drive, matching the dining-room one, and two french windows opening on to the flagged terrace overlooking the Italian garden.

As you entered there stood on your left a choice little mahogany bureau of about 1790 which had been in my father's family for many years and was always called the 'Garrick cabinet'. Too late to have had anything to do with the actor himself, it had perhaps been bought at Mrs Garrick's sale in the early nineteenth century. It was of beautiful workmanship, with a writing-slide which pulled out while the rounded cover disappeared inside, and it still had the original sand and inkpots. Being too small for serious writing it had remained in admirable condition and was only used for the display of Japanese ivory figures and netsuke on its glazed shelves. These used to be brought out so that we could see the wonderful detail in the faces of the two old men eating shellfish, the women playing with babies and the craftsmen making masks. On the underside of the bases, normally unseen, were carved the soles of these people's feet. My parents did not go in for collecting things of any one kind but there was a cult of 'japonaiserie' at about the time they married and they must have acquired them then unless they inherited them. In the bow-window recess, which had a cushioned seat following its curve, was a satinwood Pembroke table on which lay delicate little objects: snuff-boxes, candlesnuffers on their own oval tray, punch spoons with slender wooden handles, a sailing ship, a jointed silver fish and the gilt and coral eighteenth-century rattle which had been treasured in my mother's family and was given to my brother as the eldest grandchild. One silver box with pierced inner lid held a morsel of sponge which exhaled a faint musty fragrance from long, long ago.

On the other side of the bow-window was a black and gold oriental lacquer chest with doors which opened to show a number of little drawers. It stood on a gilt seventeenth-century English stand, elaborately carved. On the top was set a fine china bowl, one of many Chinese export ones which we had. Between the two french windows was a fine satinwood Georgian bureau, usually kept shut but when open revealing a series of drawers with ivory knobs. The plainness of its square top was relieved by a bronze Chinese dragon with a little detachable one on its back. In the glazed upper part were green, white and gold plates, two red oriental pots with lids and some figurines. My mother sometimes wrote at this table in the summer but she much preferred her bureau in the hall with all its familiar equipment. The drawers underneath held various games of a rather fragile kind which we never played in other rooms. Especially was there the papier-mâché box with scalloped edges and a romantic scene in glowing colours on the lid. This contained five inner boxes which all came out separately, and in these were the incomprehensible cards of some ancient game and a lot of beautiful mother-of-pearl counters. Some were sharp-pointed ovals representing fish, others of different sizes were circular, but all were covered with engraved designs. No one understood the game but we often played with the counters and when older would use them for any mild gambles. Other decorous games we played here, usually when there were visitors, were Happy Families, the Geography game which was a version of the former, and Wordmaking and Wordtaking, for which we used the much-worn

Drawing-room fireside

pasteboard letter-squares with which we had learnt to read. This was
played with a venom which grew ever fiercer as our vocabularies began
to match up to those of the grown-ups. The chair for the bureau was a
satinwood one with cane seat and a loose cushion. Two other smaller
chairs stood near and these were of similar Regency date, crested with
Prince of Wales' feathers, caned, with tie-on squab cushions.

When we first went to the house there were communicating doors
between the three rooms in this range but as my father's collection of
books in the middle room grew the doors were locked and the recesses
on his side filled with shelves. This left, in the drawing-room, a
round-headed alcove in front of which stood a three-tiered slender
mahogany whatnot. There would be flowers on the top shelf, with
framed photographs, ashtrays, a paper-knife, various ornamental trifles
and pretty illustrated books on the others. The basket grate in the north
wall was of Adam design, in a silvery metal called armourbright,
surrounded by a modern white-painted chimneypiece in the same style.
The mantelshelf held groups of mythological figures mostly of modern
Dresden, and a gilt striking clock. We had some familiarity with the
drawing-room china ornaments because it was the periodic task of the
schoolroom to wash them very carefully in hot water and Lux. Above

the fireplace hung a big gilt mirror in the Chippendale taste but known to be a reproduction. The fire was fierce when made up for a party, and beside it stood two antique pole screens with oval shields, of which the delicate original needlework had been carefully preserved with criss-crossings of stitching. On the far side of the fireplace was a mahogany Georgian card table standing against the wall with its flap closed, and for games this would be moved into the middle of the room and opened out. In the corner was another whatnot, a slenderer satinwood one, on which stood a fine Lowestoft jug.

Occupying much of the long east wall was a satinwood bow-fronted commode painted by or in the style of Angelica Kauffmann. It had good cupboards, but for fear of damage these were not much used and the only thing I can remember being brought out from them was the long lacquer box containing an enchanting Chinese fan, painted with little figures each with an ivory face stuck on. The sticks were of different materials and colours, with a pierced design, and when the fan was closed you saw a filigree dragon on the outside. Next came a satinwood chest the top of which opened to form a dressing-table, and then we return to the entrance door, masked by a six-leaved Chinese lacquer screen, probably nineteenth-century, with a cream ground and mysterious scenes from some unknown story.

I have so far described the outer edges of the room, furnished with the fine period pieces for which, to their advantage and ours, Malletts of Bath had inspired my father's enthusiasm during a convalescence in about 1915. The floor was of parquet, displayed in a generous area round the mainly brownish Persian carpet in the middle of the room, easily rolled up for dancing. On the carpet were arranged an enor-mous sofa with high back and arms, two big armchairs and other smaller ones, all loose-covered in floral chintz. A long low stool could be moved up to the fire and there were occasional tables, footstools and standard lamps. A white-painted panelled dado went about four feet up the walls, which were papered above that in a pale unemphatic damask design. The pictures were all colour prints most of which seemed to me to illustrate silly subjects, such as elaborately hatted women named after the seasons, other scantily-draped ones engaged in curious occupations such as selling cupids, and sissy children chasing butterflies in an unbusinesslike way. The white ceiling was ornamented with the plaster garlands which my mother had seen being modelled, and from its centre hung a splendid crystal chandelier of which I never heard the provenance.

Either because it seemed uncomfortably isolated from the rest of the house by its double doors, or because it was difficult to heat until the curtains had been drawn across the big windows, their blinds lowered and internal shutters closed, we used this room comparatively little. When as small children we went down after tea to play with my mother we were nearly always in the hall, where we could run about. In the drawing-room we sat on shiny chintz, cold to the backs of bare knees, and played quiet games sitting round a table, or were allowed to handle the fascinating objects from the silver table, to have the Chinese fan opened for us and look at the picture books. Yet it looked welcoming enough and must have been wonderfully characteristic of the gracious Edwardian neo-Georgian taste, warmed by personal touches. The curtains, which had started as blue, soon turned grey in spite of the outer sunblinds on the terrace, contained on rollers in boxes over the terrace windows, and pulled down with a hooked pole on hot days. There were bright colours everywhere, in the chintzes, china, flowers and prints, but nothing jumped out and there was a subtle harmony between them, a matter of instinctive taste, I think, rather than of deliberate intention. Everything was in good order but nothing ever looked new, and if a few changes were made over the years they were too slight and too gradual to notice. Whether the room influenced deportment or deportment the room I do not know but I can never remember raised voices or anything remotely sensational happening amid the soothing fragrance of flowers and furniture polish.

A door in the northwest corner of the hall opened into a lobby from which a side door led out to the kitchen garden. This was not much used and was kept carefully locked with a big key which needed two small hands to turn it. An internal wooden shutter, secured by handscrews, fitted the upper glazed portion and was put up at night, reinforced by a heavy chain. This excellent door, probably the only burglarproof item in the house, was made in a slight curve, as though it had at one time been in a bow front, but whether it had always belonged to our house or had been imported from another it is impossible to say. On the left as you entered from the hall was an immensely heavy bronze gong, about two feet in diameter, hung from a sturdy mahogany stand. For breakfast, luncheon and dinner the butler or footman would set the hall door open and beat a slow tattoo round the outer edge of the gong with a chamois-leather-covered drumstick. This required the same kind of skill as the bulb motorhorn did, for you had to let one boom nearly die away before starting another and our fetish of punctuality demanded that everyone should hear the gong wherever he or she might be.

On the right was a long built-in cupboard for overcoats with a curtained ledge above for men's hats. The bowlers, soft felts and cloth caps in everyday use just lay there and were brushed when necessary. Top hats, no longer worn very frequently, were kept in their own boxes – my father's stout hunting one with its ring for a cord guard; those used for funerals, weddings or the Eton and Harrow match at Lords; and the grey one worn sometimes for that and sometimes for weddings. My father also had an opera hat for going out in the evening in London. It was shaped like a topper but was made of dull corded silk and could be folded flat for putting under a theatre seat. To open it you pressed springs which made a characteristic clonk and this, together with the irresistibly comic nature of the whole proceeding, was perhaps why an unorthodox neighbour was much disapproved of for wearing one at funerals. The long silk pile of an ordinary black top hat was surprisingly durable; it could be washed in soap and water after hunting and smoothed with a special curved iron. They also served as crash helmets but if you concertinaed one it had to go and be reblocked, a horrid expense for girls on an exiguous dress allowance.

The righthand end of the cupboard held the overcoats and mackintoshes in constant use. My parents each had several of varying weights, from the fur or furlined ones for driving in winter to thick cloth and tweed, and light ones intended for keeping out dust from unmetalled roads rather than for warmth. My mother also used a motoring veil for this purpose, of grey chiffon gathered round a button at the top and parting in front when not required to cover the face. My father had a heavy and totally impervious mackintosh, fitted with sundry straps, surviving from his hunting days, and both he and my mother had 'Burberries'. These, invented by the firm of that name, never satisfactorily imitated and still much the same, were alike for men and women. They were of a greenish or brownish proofed material, lined either with shot silk or checked woollen, and hung loosely from the shoulders without a belt. Little buttoned tabs enabled the collar to be fastened high round the throat in a downpour or cuffs to be tightened to keep out drips. The pockets were made in the lining, unattached to the outer slits through which you reached them, and most things would keep dry in them. These coats were intensely practical and were used all the year round. As they began to get really shabby, garments would get shunted from the righthand to the lefthand end of the cupboard, but it was almost impossible to wear such things out so they remained until lack of space or a major jumble sale enforced a purge. For years a dark green check Inverness cape hung there and I cannot imagine who had ever worn it.

In the bottom of the cupboard, below the coats, were galoshes and snowboots. The former were of shiny rubber, usually black but sometimes brown, shaped like a slipper with a high tongue in front, and were pulled on over your shoes or boots, a sensible arrangement but for some reason wildly unpopular with children, who regarded them as sissy and resented their tendency to come off during strenuous activity. We had some justification in that only over-careful and fussy grown-ups wore them, and snowboots were more acceptable. These were made of black cloth with rubber soles, put on over ordinary shoes but extending above the ankle and fastened with a clasp. Both were virtually superseded by rubber wellington boots, which I first saw when I was about eleven. These, of shiny rubber, worn over socks, not shoes, had wide tops ending just below the knee and immediately became so popular that ingenuity was switched from finding excuses for not wearing galoshes to producing reasons for the boots. The prospects of rain and mud were stressed instead of the fineness of the day.

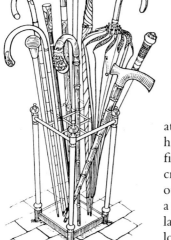

Beside the cupboard stood a well-filled brass-railed umbrella stand, divided into sections and fitted with a drip tray. This held my parents' leather-seated shooting sticks, their cane-handled black silk umbrellas from Briggs, gilt-banded and initialled, and a variety of walking sticks. The ones in most use were stout ashplants but there were several old-fashioned ones with elaborate handles of horn or damascene work which were seldom taken out. Opposite the cupboard was a rack attached to the wall, for hunting-crops. These had cane or leather-covered stocks about fifteen inches long with a roughened horn crook at one end, for opening gates. At the other was a leather loop to which was knotted a plaited leather thong, fitted at the end with a lash in bright-coloured silk, about nine inches long. The loop was doubled over and kept in

Umbrella stand in lobby

place by a rubber band so that the whip hung neatly from a stud in the rack. Although you hardly ever needed to crack a whip you were taught how to do it as a matter of course.

Next to this rack was a telephone, installed when we went to the house in 1913. It was a wooden box attached to the wall, with the vulcanite mouthpiece and receiver lying on a rest at the top. To hear, or to hear better, you squeezed a spring in the bar connecting the mouthpiece and receiver, and before you made a call you wound a handle on the right side of the box. I think this was the procedure, but I can hardly ever have used this instrument because it was replaced in the 1920s by a pillar model standing on a table. With this the mouthpiece was part of the stand and the receiver a trumpet-shaped object on a hook. As few neighbours or tradesmen had telephones at first ours was seldom used, and normal communications were carried on through the three daily posts or notes sent by hand. Also there was for some reason great resistance by my parents to the use of the telephone. I do not know whether they disliked it because it was in a uniquely cold, public and inconvenient place, or whether they put it there because they disliked it. The men's lavatory was nearby and my father hated being seen going in or out of it. I do not know whether it was worse for him listening in an agony of impatience till we had done talking to our friends or for us knowing that he must be hearing every word we said. We were all grown-up before an extension was fitted upstairs, no doubt immensely increasing the telephone bills which, in a far from cheese-paring establishment, aroused a surprising amount of resentment.

From the uncarpeted lobby a passage with a red, blue and green Turkey rug led to the door of the smoking-room and to the billiard-room at the end. The gun-cupboard, always locked, stood here, containing my father's pair of double-barrelled twelve-bore shotguns, my brother's single one at a later stage, and a .22 rifle for rooks or rabbits. A supply of cartridges and the leather bags used for carrying them over the shoulder when out shooting were kept in here too. My father was at one time a very heavy smoker and got through numerous boxes of Turkish cigarettes which came in black rectangular tins with the picture of a camel on them. They were just the right size for the pound of butter which used to be sent regularly to my brother at his preparatory school during the stringencies of the war.

After my father gave up smoking owing to incipient bronchitis it seemed more suitable to call his room the library, but somehow the new name never stuck. A big dropfront Chippendale bureau on the left of this room had a cupboard in the lower part for files, old receipts and other domestic papers. The desk part was never used but the glazed shelves above contained a quantity of books, mostly in sets. There was all of Jane Austen, half-bound in dark green; Anthony Trollope's *Barchester* series in limp green leather; Boswell's *Life of Johnson* and the *Tour of the Hebrides*, in calf; the works of Pope, Swift, Sterne, and most of the English major poets; a handsome edition of George Eliot, half-bound in red, and at the top some miscellaneous items small enough to fit into a very low shelf. Next came the locked drawing-room door, covered by shelves mainly of history and biography including the works of Lord Morley, Cunningham's edition of Horace Walpole's Letters, Lytton Strachey's *Queen Victoria* and *Eminent Victorians*, and Trevelyan's books on the Risorgimento. At right angles, in another set of shelves, were the works of Bryce and the many green volumes of a translation of St Simon's *Memoirs*; a life of Danton and other books on the French Revolution, which my father studied in some depth. There were also an old edition of the *Encyclopaedia Britannica* and several dictionaries, including that of the Académie Française. Inconspicuous on the lowest shelf were some books which he probably preferred we should not read though we were never forbidden anything. These included Michael Arlen's *Green Hat*, works of Havelock Ellis and an unedifying volume of potted biographies of Roman empresses.

In the window stood a big mahogany roll-top desk with a delicate tambour cover which had to be raised very evenly to make it disappear smoothly into its allotted space. My father was tidy and did not hoard, but out of the little drawers he used to produce old seals, miniature photographs and obsolete patent pens, evidently kept for sentiment, as well as such useful equipment as a compass or the wheel for measuring distances on maps. The desk was kept closed, with a few drawers locked, but on the whole secrecy was frowned upon, and I imagine he kept really confidential papers in his office. On the top stood a barograph, of which he changed the chart regularly, a bronze bust of Napoleon on a yellow marble stand and a small replica of Houdon's statue of Voltaire in the Comédie Française. His writing chair was an early nineteenth-century cross-framed one with a cane seat. On the far side of the window was a settee against the wall and more bookshelves above it. Here there were sets of Thackeray, Thomas Hardy, Rudyard Kipling, Galsworthy and some bestsellers of their day: Hutchinson's *If Winter Comes*, Keynes' *Economic Consequences of the Peace*, Childers' *Riddle of the Sands*, and beautiful illustrated editions of John Masefield's *Right Royal* and *Reynard the Fox*. Other shelves, at right angles, blocked the door into the billiard-room and in these were a whole set of the works of O. Henry, an author much relished by my father; several volumes of the Badminton Library on field sports; Fortescue's *Story of a Red Deer*, which was often read aloud to us, and many works on horses, their care, training and cure. At the bottom there was space for very large illustrated books, of which I remember Slipper's *ABC of Sport*, *The Three Jovial Huntsmen* with Caldecott's illustrations, and Grimm's *Fairy Tales*. The chimneypiece was early nineteenth-century, of veined grey marble, very plain, with a mirror in a simple moulded gilt frame above it. An old striking clock stood on the mantelshelf with bronzes on either side. The low grate, with its moulded curb, always in winter had a good fire burning ready for my father's return from London at 6.30, but it was not lit till about 5 and if you wanted a book during the day you almost needed to put on an overcoat to get it. The fire was replenished from a wooden scuttle with a tin lining which was exchanged for a full one when emptied, the menservants coming in from time to time to see to this.

On the other side of the fireplace were mainly topographical books, the delightful Neale's *Seats*, and some histories of Essex. In the corner, on a small sturdy antique mahogany table, stood a press from which my father could take copies of letters in purple ink on flimsy paper. When this method became obsolete the little table was exchanged for a fine Irish Chippendale card table on which usually lay some newly acquired books. Along the fourth wall, up to the door, was a large mahogany Georgian break-front bookcase in which nearly all the books were bound or half-bound handsomely in leather. Here were sets of Dickens, Walter Scott and Surtees, Prescott, Motley, Grote, and Gibbon's *Decline and Fall of the Roman Empire*. On a tall shelf were illustrated books on furniture, such as *The Age of Satinwood* and others of that series. The floor, with an edge of polished oak showing, was covered with a worn tawny Turkey carpet, and in front of the fire were two armchairs upholstered with eastern carpet saddlebags in predominantly red and blue. On the fine piecrust mahogany revolving table would be cigarettes, the cutter for the cigars which were kept in a cupboard in the big bookshelf, books in the course of being read, and two or three paper-knives. At that time most new books were uncut when bought and there was a voluptuous pleasure in skimming the contents while operating on the pages with a silver, ivory or tortoiseshell knife. This was supposed to be done all at one time, a piecemeal cutting while reading being thought a careless habit.

The billiard-room at the far end of the passage was used a great deal when we first went to the house, especially by men staying in the house or dining. From an early age we were trained to listen for the shot before going in. The green felt-covered table on solid bulbous legs took up most of the space and the sides of the room were left unencumbered, though comfortably carpeted with Turkey rugs. At one end was a modern fireplace surrounded by a leather-covered settle and at the other, in the window embrasure, a big upholstered seat on a dais for spectators of the game. The dais itself was moveable and would be taken into the dining-room window recess at Christmas when we acted plays written for us by our governess. On the garden side two french windows opened on to the terrace and between them was fixed to the wall a marker for scoring, and two rollers which clicked round showing the appropriate figures. During the 1914–18 war wounded soldiers used to come from a local hospital for tea and billiards. They looked incredibly clean in their bright blue flannel suits, white shirts and red ties, hopping nimbly around on crutches or using the rests to do the work of a bandaged or missing hand. As time went on, however, orthodox billiards became less popular and we more often played frivolous versions with the multi-coloured composition balls kept in bottle-shaped wicker containers, stowed in a corner near the stand for cues and rests. The two white and one red ivory balls for the serious game were kept resting in cotton wool in a leather box on the chimneypiece. Inevitably, the little-used billiard-room became a repository for all sorts of large objects and we kept here the croquet set with which we played a much-debased game, sometimes by torchlight or moonlight on summer nights, with mallets muffled in dusters so as not to wake my parents.

Seven

THE BEST BEDROOMS

Over the billiard-room was the 'pink room', one of the prettiest in the house but icily cold in winter from the windows on two sides, facing north and west. In summer, however, visitors could enjoy the scent of the wistaria which climbed up to them, and the lovely view of the Italian garden and the wood beyond. It had a double bed with railed mahogany head and foot, and covered with a pink eiderdown and bedspread. On the marble mantelshelf were china figures and a set of Worcester vases, and in winter a fire would be kept burning here for much of the day. The marble-topped washstand was equipped with a jug, basin, toothbrush dish and soapdish ornamented with pink roses on a white ground, and in the cupboard beside the bed was a chamber-pot of the same pattern for use in the night. A visitor

Bedroom jug and basin

sleeping here would be expected only to use the bathroom for having a bath, and a brass can of hot water, covered with a towel, would be stood in the basin before breakfast, luncheon and dinner, and at bedtime.

In the window was a rather questionably antique mahogany dressing-table with an undeniably period looking-glass standing on it. The guest's own dressing-set of two hair-brushes, one or two clothes brushes, a hand mirror and a variety of pots and jars would be set out on a white linen table runner. Although these made the luggage very heavy it was essential for prestige purposes to carry the whole equipment, often very pretty, in silver, ivory, enamel or tortoiseshell. A hanging-wardrobe, a chest of drawers, a small fully equipped writing-table, two cane-seated chairs and one little chintz-covered armchair completed the furnishings. The floral curtains were predominantly pink, carrying on the theme of the room. The adjoining dressing-room communicated by means of a double door, one felt-covered, the other panelled. In practice these two rooms were seldom used as a suite, the smaller one being for years my brother's bedroom. It contained a single bed, a man's wardrobe with space for hanging jackets in the upper part, a high dressing-table, to be used while standing, and the inevitable marble-topped washstand with all accoutrements.

These rooms opened on to a long corridor, covered like the front stairs in a chocolate-brown pile carpet, the walls hung with a miscellaneous collection of old sepia or black-and-white prints, in black frames with gilt slips. My father's room came next and as he was a bad sleeper who read for much of the night he had a bookshelf near his outsize single bed with mahogany head and foot. There was an oak tallboy of which, being very tall himself, he could conveniently use all the drawers. He had a boot-cupboard containing about twenty pairs of boots and shoes, all most beautifully made for him by a firm called Taylor. There were black boots with grey cloth tops for formal wear; leather ones for every day; several pairs of brown shoes of varying weights for country wear; shooting boots – greased instead of polished; white buckskin tennis shoes with rubber soles, and patent-leather pumps for evening dress, with low fronts and little black bows. As time went on he gave up boots except for shooting but always kept in his room an old pair of gloves to use when putting on and lacing up footwear. Unlike our more ordinary shoes, which were polished by the houseboy with Kiwi or Cherry Blossom in an outside boot-hole, my father's were done in the pantry by the butler, with browning or blacking from an earthenware bottle. The syrupy liquid was applied with a stick and then rubbed in and burnished with a stag- or beef-bone to produce a deep gloss which, considering all the work that went into it, was surprisingly vulnerable. Puppies had to be taught very early not to lick it, something they all wanted to do because, I strongly suspect, it contained some ingredient to which they could become addicted. Beside the high mahogany dressing-table in the window stood a round Victorian shaving-mirror, which could be turned to the light on its own stand. My father shaved with a set of cut-throat razors, each marked with a day of the week. They were kept in a locked case and he honed them himself on a leather strap which hung on the window-frame.

A big mahogany wardrobe and a built-in cupboard held his many suits: the evening tails, dinner-jacket and velvet smoking-jacket; morning tailcoat and striped trousers; black jackets and striped trousers such as he wore every day at the office; dark formal suits, smooth tweed ones and the rougher shooting-jackets and knicker-bockers; grey flannels for summer and white ones for tennis; the dark blue blazer with gilt buttons which he wore at Henley Regatta along with the pink tie, socks and hat-ribbon of the Leander Club. He also had an immense quantity of shirts and underwear because, at least when at home, he never wore any linen more than once before it went to be laundered. His suits came first from Lesley and Roberts, then from Davis; his hats from Hillhouse, and shirts, which were always made for him, from Beale and Inman.

He looked well-groomed and clean to a degree which was remark-able even among his exact compeers but never appeared to be wearing anything actually new. He always seemed to have been wearing the same clothes, and indeed with so many it must have been difficult to wear them out. His unhurried neat movements were probably good for clothes. He would take his gold half-hunter repeater watch out of his waistcoat pocket with unruffled calm at all times, because with his habitual punctuality he can hardly ever have had the shock of finding it was later than he thought. His monocle, unassisted by such aids as a cord or metal frame, stayed firmly in place held only by its milled edge, unless he raised an eyebrow and dropped the glass out to polish it, or replace it with pince-nez for reading or steel-rimmed spectacles for games. Only towards the end of his life did he take to wearing tortoiseshell-rimmed spectacles at all times; by which date he had also given up the black jacket and striped trousers in favour of suits, and had totally abandoned boots. He needed an hour and a half to drink early morning tea, bathe, shave and dress, so was always called at 6.30 for breakfast at 8. When he occasionally came down late it was because he had cut himself with his lethal razors, blobs of cotton wool betraying the mishap, which must on no account be commented on.

My father's room had a door opening into a bathroom between it and my mother's. It was a converted bedroom with a marble chimneypiece and grate in it and, like most bathrooms of that date, had a bell for use in emergency. One major emergency was indeed connected with it, for my father was operated on for appendicitis there in 1914. The nurse who looked after him must have been a retired or seconded Army Sister because when she came out for walks with the nursery party she wore a smart little scarlet cape. With her uniform and piles of white hair she was very impressive and there was no nonsense of any kind from anyone when she was around.

The bathroom was probably rather luxurious for its time. The floor was in diagonal black and bluish-white tiles of some kind of rubbery material, warmer to the feet than ordinary linoleum. The taps had handles of ivory or a good imitation of it and the waste was operated by a stopper which pulled up a tube from the level of the taps. There was a wash-basin which my mother and the governess used instead of having cans brought to their bedrooms, and a large weighing machine which had a pile of graduated weights for the stones, with an indicator you moved along an arm to show the ounces. As small children we hardly ever went to this bathroom except for the weighing ceremony, which was done regularly and rather more often than the marking of our heights in pencil on the jamb of the nursery door. Like all the rooms in the house this bathroom was kept immaculately clean but if you had seen it just after my father had used it in the morning you would have got a shock, and the governess once nearly fainted. For washing he had a wooden bowl of soap about ten inches in diameter and a stiff brush made of vegetable bristles. He worked up a tremendous lather with which he covered himself all over and then, only then, did he get into the bath to remove it. He explained the process to me once in some indignation when I ventured to ask him how he made such a mess. The idea of doing the soaping in the bath and then wallowing in the same water would, he said, be unbelievably disgusting. The lather flew everywhere, often reaching the ceiling, and was a delicate pink if he had cut himself shaving, or spinach-green if he had been using a plaster for lumbago.

My mother's room also communicated with this bathroom and was directly over the drawing-room. It therefore had a similar big bow-window, with a low sill guarded by an iron grille, and it looked over the drive with a side view of the top of the rose-covered pergola from which delicious scents blew in. There was a grey carpet, striped grey and white wallpaper and faded blue curtains. The seemingly enormous double bed was unbelievably soft compared to our nursery ones, and one or other of us was allowed to share it during alarming thunderstorms. A phenomenon I classed with these, though they did not last long enough to alter sleeping arrangements, were zeppelin and aeroplane raids of the 1914–18 war, heralded always by the screeching of cock pheasants. I was surprised when, on a visit to an aunt in Surrey, I was flatteringly pressed to describe them. Up till then I had supposed they were of the natural order of things and that everyone had had them.

At the foot of my mother's bed was an ottoman, an upholstered box which doubled as a sofa and for storing such things as old lace and evening wraps. The big dressing-table was a converted Georgian sideboard, its top covered with a sheet of plate glass on which stood an antique mahogany-framed mirror with little drawers at the foot. Her ivory brushes, with her monogram in black, fitted into a crocodile-leather dressing-case for travelling. Among the appointments of this beautifully made but fiendishly heavy piece of luggage were the little spirit lamp and tongs with which she curled her quasi-Edwardian fringe. She had the usual marble-topped washstand and a cupboard especially made for numerous pairs of shoes. There were two or three light cane-seated bedroom chairs. A very big wardrobe, occupying all one wall, held most of her clothes but there was also an antique mahogany serpentine-fronted chest of drawers. On the Adam-style mantelshelf stood a white china goat, a much-loved souvenir of her finishing-school period in Dresden, and various little animals, mostly dogs, in painted bronze. The fender had a brightly polished brass edge and enclosed the brass fire utensils which were in fairly frequent use, as a fire would be lit on winter evenings for any elaborate dressing. Her dressing-gown would be laid over an armchair beside it and her quilted silk bedroom slippers set near.

On the wall were pictures of favourite horses and of Little Bookham Manor, her grandfather's house which she regarded more as home than her parents', which changed fairly often. A reproduction of a painting by Lucy Kemp-Welch, whom they had known, and representing a horsefair I think, had a place of honour, for my mother had learnt to paint horses rather well herself and much admired this artist, as she did Rosa Bonheur. Next to the bathroom door hung a little shelf, my brother's first usable production in the carpentry he loved, and on this were arranged the crested china ornaments, mostly made by Goss, which we used to bring her as presents from the seaside. Her own natural tidiness and the attentions of the head housemaid who looked after her things ensured that one very seldom caught the room in disarray, and nothing in it ever seemed to change.

I find it difficult to remember much detail of my mother's clothes, perhaps because she always had an unemphatic elegance which suited

her trim unchanging figure and her capacity for 'taking on the colour
of the landscape', as people like us assiduously tried to do. I think of
her as looking much the same over the years but this must be
erroneous for she loved clothes and had a great many, to please both
herself and my father, who was very observant of what his women-
folk wore. I recall that when we first went to Pilgrims' Hall her
daytime clothes were longer and darker than they were later, and that
in winter she often put on a voluminous nutria fur coat or a black
sealskin one. She also had a sable stole, with tails hanging down, and a
sumptuous muff to match. Muffs were a great comfort to children as
well as to their owners since cold and invariably chilblained hands
could be taken in and warmed up during winter walks and drives. Her
evening dresses, which at that date I seldom saw, were soft, flowing
and shimmery, a great contrast to the harsh starchy textures of our
nursery world. She must have bought few clothes during the war and
was usually in a tweed coat and skirt, with the skirt ample enough for
bicycling. When social life revived, and particularly in the late 1920s
when some of us were growing up, she again bought beautiful
dresses. They were made for her by two French sisters, the Mesdemoiselles Lehmann in Wigmore Street, who had hived off from her
former dressmaker, Handley Seymour. Her shoes were hand-made
for her by the firm which made my father's, and her suits came from
the tailor, Daniel Thomas of South Molton Street, who also made her
side-saddle riding-habits.

Various friends and relations used to take moors for shooting in
Scotland and it was customary to buy lengths of tweed when staying
with them, or to receive them as presents. The ones my mother chose
were soft in colour and feel, never loudly patterned, and lasted for
years. Dress materials were of pure wool, or silk in its various
manifestations of chiffon and crêpe-de-chine, and in summer there
would emerge cottons in pastel shades or the bolder striped Maccles-
field silks. She had a fresh natural colour, using no make-up except
powder for her nose, refreshed discreetly when out with 'papiers
poudrés' from her handbag. Her finer jewellery – a diamond pendant
given her by my father when my brother was born, and a diamond
rivière inherited from my grandmother – she wore of course only in
the evening. In daytime she had a single string of pearls, sometimes a
pearl and diamond bar brooch and, most often, a small watch in a blue
enamel and diamond case on a chain round her neck. She could not see
the time from it unless she put on reading glasses and in fact she never

went much by watches at all. I think she relied on the chiming clocks and the regular noises of the house by which we knew without thinking approximately what the time was. There was the gong for meals, the bell for the maids' elevenses, the separator starting up in the dairy at 4 pm, and the uncanny silence which descended on the back regions in the early afternoon when all housework was finished.

A door led out of my mother's room to the corridor with a lavatory nearby, situated over the men's one on the ground floor and equally liable to freeze up. A very steep flight of eight steps went down to the main landing and front stairs, an inconvenient device for giving height to the drawing-room. Up and down these were carried, year in, year out, the early morning or guests' breakfast trays, coals, hot water, or slops for emptying, with hardly ever an accident. On the left of the landing was a door leading to a linoleum-floored subsidiary passage on which opened a housemaids' pantry, a lavatory and bathroom. In the pantry were cleaning materials for this part of the house, a row of brightly polished brass hot-water cans and larger brown-painted ones for the bedrooms. Two or three cylindrical earthenware hot-water bottles with screw stoppers were kept here for airing beds but we did not provide any of the more luxurious indiarubber ones for guests. We expected to take our own with us when travelling. Enamel slop-pails stood ready for the emptying of wash-basins and chamber-pots in bedrooms, and a sluice arrangement dealt with these in this pantry. The lavatory like all others in the house had a varnished wooden seat and an overhead cistern worked by a ball and chain, the latter striking you a sharp blow on the back of the head if you left it swinging as you went out. The bathroom had a nice rubber floor like my parents' one but otherwise was cheerless, with no hand-basin and a too-big bath which chilled the unreliable hot water.

Two windows lighted the landing and there were three good cupboards in the thickness of the walls. One held unused lamps, games and old toys; another our riding clothes and boots, the latter on their heavy wooden trees, with the bootjack for getting the boots off, and hooks and 'jockey' for putting them on – this was a grooved metal plate which enabled you to pull the boot over your breeches without rucking the legs up. On shelves in the third cupboard were some simple medicines such as aspirin, Syrup of Figs and Eno's Fruit Salts, the best toilet soap, bought in bulk from the Army and Navy Stores, and packets of Bromo toilet paper. The rolls of Bronco, for the staff and for children not yet given the freedom of the front of the house, were kept elsewhere. A coarse Dutch marquetry cupboard, two reproduction Chippendale stools and a fine old grandfather clock furnished the landing. For our first few years a local watchmaker, Mr Lemmon, used to come out once a week to wind all the clocks but after a time my father took over and always did them between breakfast and church on Sundays. We had many good antique ones and their different strikes going off within a few seconds of each other seemed both to regulate and confirm the orderliness of the house.

The front stairs had a nicely moulded rail and balustrade on the right side as you went up and on the left was a long strip of wall on which hung the three oars won by my brother in a successful college rowing career at Oxford. The blades were painted dark blue with the University College crest and the names and weights of the crews in gold. At the top of the stairs a door on the left opened into the room which was at first my mother's 'boudoir' and then became the schoolroom. This will be described in the following chapter and we will pass on to the governess's bedroom beyond it. This was small but nicely furnished with a good mahogany wardrobe, chest of drawers, washstand and dressing-table. What we did not unfortunately know till long afterwards was that Miss Salisbury, who was with us for many years, never dared to have the window open at night. She thought that some intruder might climb up the iron balcony outside and get in, a fear we children can have done nothing to dispel because we frequently climbed up this balcony ourselves. No one else ever thought of such things as burglaries and nocturnal prowlings, but she was perfectly right and the room was much more suitable for my brother, who took it over when the schoolroom régime ended. Our insensitivity and her reluctance to complain appals me, looking back on it now.

At the eastern end of the landing were five steps, not so steep as the ones already described but serving the same purpose of giving height to the room below. At their head three doors opened on to a small landing. Behind the one on the right was a ladder up to the loft used as a boxroom and above it, at the side, were doors through which trunks could be lowered. The boxroom itself was a fascinating place, part of it boarded over but the rest left as the rough lath and plaster of the ceilings below, through which we were warned we should fall if we set foot there. The huge tanks, equally out of bounds, were reached up some subsidiary steps, and a trapdoor led out on to the roof where we went fairly often. We were trusted not to get into danger but forbidden to stamp or jump about for fear of making depressions where rain would settle on the leads. The house on the whole was tidy and unwanted objects were removed smartly, but no one bothered much about the loft where there was space enough for anything. There were of course the trunks in common use, my father's big leather one and a leather suitcase, both very heavy even when empty. My mother had a lighter trunk, covered in green canvas, and also what she called her bonnet-box, made square and deep for hats which could be pinned to pads on the sides. The maids had either wicker boxes, consisting of two deep trays fitting together and secured with a strap, or tin trunks painted mottled brown.

Most remarkable was the nursery luggage, brought down several days before we went to the seaside. The major items were a huge dark brown leather trunk and the bath. The latter was oval, painted like the maids' tin trunks in mottled brown, and with a lid which strapped on. Nanny used to fill it with all the heaviest things – the boots and shoes, buckets and spades, camp stools and rugs – until it took at least two strong men to lift it. Not only was it heavy but it was villainously slippery as well and had no carrying handles. Porters used to groan mutinously as they tried to hoist it on to the waggonette hired from Thomas Tilling to transport us from Liverpool Street to a Southern Railway terminus but Nanny, usually so retiring, kept them at it with the utmost determination and at the end probably tipped them far too little. She had of course a proprietary interest in the London, Brighton and South Coast railway because her eldest brother, Jesse, drove one of its cream-and-chocolate engines and he might always have been driving us, though I do not remember that he ever did. All the same he sent my brother and me each a dark blue enamelled can with a cup which fitted over the top and a dropdown handle, such as was taken on the footplate by drivers and firemen. These came in handy for innumerable games.

The rooms we went to for years at Littlehampton were kept by a retired fisherman, Mr Horne, his wife and schoolteacher daughter, and they were Nanny's special friends. The rooms were tiny, crowded with heavy Victorian furniture, the chimneypiece draped with green plush, scalloped at the edge and decorated with chenille bobbles. There was probably no bathroom but if there had been it would not have been let to us so we had our famous travelling bath and a small one for the baby on its own stand. Everything was always slightly gritty from the sand we brought in on our shoes and clothes from the

beach, and the food was different from what we had at home. We had
shrimps sometimes for tea, instead of jam, and Cadbury's chocolate
biscuits packed, as many things were in those patriotic days, in red,
white and blue wrappings. Relaxed as the discipline was, however, we
were never allowed on the beach on Sundays, but used to go for
decorous walks in the town in tidy clothes, and in the evening gather
round the daughter of the house, who played and sang hymns for us at
the piano in the front room. She stood no nonsense from us, and when
a violent quarrel developed one breakfast-time as to who should have
which of the different, fascinating and unfamiliar egg-cups, she
emerged like a tornado from the kitchen region and swept them all
away.

Cumbrous as was the nursery luggage it was more manageable than
some of the long-disused trunks which also had a place in the
boxroom. Two had domed lids, and inner trays stiffened with cane,
and they were covered in pictorial labels from Italian and French
hotels, Venice, Cadenabbia, Monaco and the like, souvenirs probably
of the extensive continental travels of my father's parents. One was
used as the dressing-up box, resorted to for charades and the
Christmas play. The major property was a complete Turkish or Greek
outfit of unknown provenance, with turned-up gold shoes, a fez, a
gold-braided and buttoned waistcoat, velvet jacket and white pleated
skirt. So desirable were these items and so much better than anything
else in the box that we always shared them out, and I do not
remember anyone ever wearing the complete costume.

The next door off the small landing was that of the biggest and best
spare-room, always called the 'green room' from its carpet, chintz
curtains and the paint of the doors and inner window-frames. It was
over the dining-room so had a corresponding bow-window, in the
recess of which stood a large mahogany dressing-table, actually a
converted sideboard. The twin beds, with mahogany rails at head and
foot, had deep box-springs from Heal's, with hair mattresses over
them, as did all the beds in the front part of the house. Only sampled
through the hospitality of a visiting aunt, or occasionally in a
convalescence, they were gloriously comfortable. The first impact of
the linen sheets, laundered to a delightful slipperiness, must have been
icy on cold nights but guests would be able to look at a bright fire in
the marble-framed fireplace. The rest of the furniture was on a big
scale: a mahogany wardrobe, a fine serpentine-fronted chest with an
escritoire top, an ample washstand with an ivy-patterned set, a settee

at the end of the beds and a substantial wing armchair. The dressing-room, opening out of it through a felt-covered door, was rather dull because its window looked out on the wall of the nursery wing, and it contained nothing but masculine furniture of a functional kind. With this room we have reached the limit of the front part of the house, and must pass through the double-leaved, leather-covered, brass-studded doors which were always kept strictly closed against noises and possible cookery smells from the very different region inhabited by domestic staff and children.

Eight

THE SCHOOLROOM

At the top of the front stairs, on the left, a white panelled door with elegant brass fittings opened into the pretty room furnished for my mother with almost exactly the same contents as the drawing-room at Warley Side. It had a parquet floor, a Persian carpet and an Adam-style chimneypiece and basket grate with a gilt mirror for overmantel. There were two windows, facing the drive, and from one of them you could walk out on to the balcony above the front porch, a point of vantage much appreciated as a place from which to watch arrivals and departures. The dogs liked this very much. Soon after our arrival formal lessons were begun for my brother and me who by this time could read although I could not yet write. A young and charming daily governess used to be brought back from Brentwood in the trap which had taken my father to the station, and as she came for mornings only the room was hardly disturbed and my mother still used it at other times. Soon, however, she had to abandon it to us and it was not until we had all left home that she started using it again and gave it back its prettiness.

When the first resident governess came the scene was transformed. A strong deal-topped table covered with a green serge cloth was put in the middle of the room with the leather-seated dining-room chairs from Warley Side ranged round it. The carpet was replaced by a more durable green one and the occasional tables and bric-à-brac were taken away. A small upright piano was imported and a blackboard and easel stood by the french window. A top central light replaced the lamps, with a weight device to enable it to be pulled down for close work, and we also had a globe.

The revolving bookcase remained and on this stood a cage for Joey, our most successful pet and one who died of old age instead of meeting the gory deaths, probably the dog's work, suffered by our white rabbit and white mice. Joey was a greenfinch whom we rescued, and he lived for about twelve years, never being able to fly because of a permanently damaged wing. He became extraordinarily tame and in the holidays his door was always left open when we were in the room. He liked perching on the rails of model trains but got nervous if long out of his cage and we fixed up a little ladder so that he could hop back in when he felt like it. He sang loudly and on the whole pleasantly but if he indulged too much in the raucous green-finch screech we used to stop him by throwing the penwiper at him. Penwipers were quite a feature of our lives. To keep a nib in good order you had to wipe it before putting the pen away and we devoted much ingenuity to making penwipers to give away as presents. There were always plenty of scraps of flannel for this purpose but we could rarely emulate the neat discs of chamois leather which, enclosed in tooled leather, were bought for parents or guests in good London shops.

In the middle of the schoolroom table stood a round lead inkstand with a wide flat base which made it impossible to upset. Under the lid were holes for pens, encircling the little white pottery inkwell which used to be filled up from a big bottle of Stephens' blue-black ink kept in the cupboard contrived out of the thickness of the wall on the left of the fireplace. Exercise books and all spare supplies of stationery were kept here too, along with the screw-topped jar of cyanide with which we killed butterflies. Our ravages on the natural world were not serious but we reared tadpoles, and collected birds' eggs, butterflies and wild flowers, lessons on them being based on specimens rather than on their habits in the wild. Books were kept in the revolving bookcase: *Our Island Story*, *Round the Wonderful World*, Chardenal's *French Exercises*, *Les Malheurs de Sophie*, *Little Arthur's England* and the cherished volumes of *Highways of History* which I collected, mainly for the illustrations. The table drawer held our flat varnished wooden rulers, penholders, boxes of Relief nibs, indiarubbers, paintboxes and beautiful pencils. The latter were always of the best quality, of pinkish fragrant cedarwood and costing fourpence each. We rang the changes on the red Royal Sovereign, the yellow Koh-i-noor and the green Venus, grade HB for writing and B for drawing.

The schoolroom was of course the governess's sitting-room so the sofa and two armchairs had been retained and she had a bureau between the windows, sometimes taking out personal treasures from it to show us. There was a pretty Adam chimneypiece with basket grate in which we used to roast chestnuts picked up in the garden and where she heated her own special iron. We did not often see her doing this because she was supposed to be relieved of our presence after tea. The iron was of bright smooth metal, of brass or the colour of brass with a little door at the back. She kept in the fire a slug of rough iron until it was red-hot and then, with the tongs from the fender, she dropped it through the little door. This excellent device made it unnecessary to clean the iron on emery paper or test it for temperature and freedom from smuts, as with the more ordinary flat-irons used by the maids.

At 11 am the footman used to bring up milk and biscuits on a tray, and 12 we broke off and were taken out for a brisk walk with the dog along the roads or, in dry weather, some of the delightful footpaths in the neighbourhood. We always met several people as most went about their business on foot and we had frequent chats with the roadman who was permanently employed filling potholes and tidying verges, his heaps of stone and earth being spaced out at frequent intervals on the roadside. We did not talk to tramps, who were on their way from the Stamford Rivers Workhouse to the Billericay one, but they sometimes said things to us, which was rather frightening. They seemed to us, and I expect really were, horrifyingly dirty and dilapidated, but some were cheerful over a fry-up in the ditch, with a pan carried about them along with other useful oddments. The governess let us bowl hoops, jump ditches, cut ourselves sticks, pretend to be horses and so forth, if we refrained from noisiness and deliberate mudlarking. We must have been well-known by sight and I have since heard, which surprises me, that we were thought to be under very strict discipline.

After luncheon at 1 o'clock we lay on our backs on the floor for half an hour while we were read to and then we went out again for another walk or to play in the garden. It had to be very wet indeed for us to stay indoors. Lessons began again at 3.30 and tea was at 5 round the schoolroom table, laid with a white cloth. We had a plate of cut bread-and-butter to start with and then slices from the loaf for jam, which was not allowed with butter. Cakes, unless somebody had recently had a birthday, were of various plain varieties including those flavoured with the hated caraway seed. When these appeared we just went without cake until the governess, who fortunately liked them, had finished. After tea we were with my mother, downstairs or in the garden, or went to the nursery where we later had supper – cocoa, Bovril or milk, with biscuits and bread-and-butter. The governess's supper was taken to the schoolroom on a tray, except on Sundays when she put on an evening dress and dined with my parents and guests.

It seems to me that what we received was not so much an education as a quite useful substitute for it. Although I did belatedly acquire university degrees true academics always smell a rat instantly and know that I am not one of them. How right indeed they are, because at the age when one should have been mopping up real knowledge like a sponge I was absorbing so much of a mixed-up and random kind. Now that everyone goes to school, and to university if possible, it seems strange that there was nothing peculiar in doing neither. I rather think that at my finishing school in Paris quite half the twenty or so pupils had learnt at home under governesses as I had. It would not, however, have been *avant garde* to have had a more formal education and I think my parents must have deliberately decided against it for some wholly benevolent reason best known to themselves. What this was I shall never know because education apparently fell into the same category as religion, money, sex and food in not ever being discussed with us.

If one considers what parents expected their children's lives to be, mine were not unreasonable. A son had to make his way in the world, but the daughter of a well-to-do, unambitious, unacademic family was likely to marry a country neighbour or businessman, a member of the more obvious professions such as the Army or Navy, or an India or colonial official. Even in poorer families she was not required to earn her living before marriage, let alone after it, and indeed the market had little use for spirited young ladies of independent means. To grind for a qualification which would enable her to take the bread out of the mouth of someone who needed it more was likely to appeal only to those with a real sense of vocation. It was still very much a man's world; before the implications of the 1914–18 war had really sunk in, accepting this might well seem to hold out more hopes of happiness than a career.

Our schoolroom, therefore, and its routine, seems very old-fashioned to look back on. We were of different ages and seldom did a lesson together. In the early days my brother, though only a year older, was being coached for his preparatory school in elementary Latin and more advanced arithmetic than seemed necessary for me.

The one who was not actually being taught had to do writing exercises or learn poetry and no excuses were tolerated for allowing oneself to be distracted. This early training in concentration was perhaps the most valuable lesson we ever had and essential when, later on, you wanted to apply your mind to something difficult while ordinary family life racketed around you. Lack of heating in any but the rooms used in common made quiet and privacy difficult to achieve in the winter. When my brother went to school Clemency Chamen, who was my own age, came to lessons with me, but while I was academically more advanced she was exceptionally musical so that her piano lessons were a background for my prep and for my younger sister learning to read and write.

Geography was taught to us all together, sometimes with the aid of the globe, but consisted of mainly learning by heart the names of countries, their capitals, principal rivers and mountains. It was a popular subject because it involved the delightful task of tracing and colouring maps, red paint being much in demand for the ubiquitous British Empire. One never expected anything to change and the transformation of St Petersburg into Petrograd took a lot of explaining. The lessons were enlivened by reading aloud in turns from a book describing the experiences of a boy, Jim, who went round the world with his tutor in a liner. Another tougher book in small print, illustrated with harsh engravings of tea-gardens, rubber plantations and so forth, drily described the characteristics and products of distant countries.

Very stupidly, we were highly resistant to French, especially to speaking it which we thought sounded silly, and as we never met any French people it remained remote from real life. The choice of books too was unfortunate because from the enjoyable *Fables* of La Fontaine in a charming illustrated edition we went on to *Les Malheurs de Sophie*. This horrid little girl represented everything we most disliked with her exhibitionism and her capacity for getting into idiotic scrapes; you would never have caught us walking in the builders' quicklime and burning our feet. Our long-suffering Miss Salisbury, I realize now, spoke French execrably herself but she had a thorough knowledge of the written language and got a great deal into our heads by plugging away at dictation and Chardenal's exercises on such things as 'la plume de ma tante'. Grammar, vocabulary and a facility in reading were there when the opportunity came to learn to speak in France.

English was taught through composition, the learning of poetry by heart and a strange exercise called parsing. This consisted of identifying

Kathleen Lawrence on her home-bred horse, Vindictive, in about 1930. The rather curious and not entirely inappropriate name commemorated that of a ship in the wartime Zeebrugge raid with which his birth had coincided. Like most of her contemporaries she rode side-saddle and the silk hat was part of the full dress of the winter season. For cub-hunting or hacking she would have worn a bowler. The collar of her dark grey habit is the blue one of the Essex Hunt

The family cars, about 1929. Bill and Lesley learned to drive on the Chevrolet, and he had it at Oxford. The Sunbeam landaulette, with its partitioned driving-seat, required the chauffeur and was used for station-work and formal occasions. Bill and Lesley were allowed to drive the Sunbeam tourer and this was used much more

Pilgrims' Hall with Bill driving the Austin Seven in the garden, against house-rules

Pilgrims' Hall, after an oil painting by Rex Whistler, 1936

the parts of speech in a sentence and writing down such comments as that so-and-so was an adjective qualifying the noun. At first it seemed mumbo-jumbo but gradually it began to make sense and had its own fascination, leading on to the rather more agreeable 'analysis' in which you ruled columns and assigned the words of a sentence to their correct categories. Our governess was unquestionably very good at explaining her criticisms of our compositions but she gave us no general introduction to literature. It was not until her successor, Miss Burton, came that I read any lyrical poetry and learned any historical sequence of authors. Recitations had previously been chosen from something like the *Lays of Ancient Rome*, *The Charge of the Light Brigade*, *The Armada* or *The Revenge*, warlike and chauvinistic as we were.

We had a daily lesson in scripture which meant reading from the bible and a fairly thorough initiation into the stories of the Old Testament and the parables of the New. We learned the Collects to be heard on Sundays but we were let off these in the holidays, so I have some permanent gaps; later, with confirmation in view, I was promoted to the history of the prayer-book from which I extracted quite a lot of meat. History was taught wholly from a British standpoint and by a series of incidents rather than in any logical progression. Foreign countries hardly existed except as our enemies or allies in war, and our knowledge of America began with Christopher Columbus and ended with the Pilgrim Fathers. Red Indians, who figured so prominently in our books and games, were never placed in a historical context or assigned any dates. Miss Salisbury was a romantic and did not care for the Hanoverians at all. We knew much more about William the Conqueror and poor Harold, Rufus' untimely end, the murder of Thomas à Becket, the unexplained fates of Henry VIII's wives, the fall of Cardinal Wolsey, the glories of Queen Elizabeth, Francis Drake and Walter Raleigh, the escapes of Charles II and Bonnie Prince Charlie than we did about laws and constitutions. In these we got no further than Magna Carta; but ask us who was drowned in a butt of Malmesey wine, what king was crowned with his mother's bracelet, who died of a surfeit of lampreys, where the Fire of London started and finished, or who was 'the little gentleman in black velvet' and we would have answered up nicely. Deficient as they obviously were, however, our history lessons were nothing if not interesting, enriched by famous pictures and ringing phrases.

Mathematics appeared so definitely not my subject that I was never taken on to algebra and geometry in the schoolroom though I tackled them with comparative ease after I grew up. There must have been something wrong with the teaching here and I think arithmetic was made too concrete. I was distracted by vivid mental pictures of taps filling cisterns, trains passing at different speeds, rooms being papered and people starting out at different times to reach their destination simultaneously. The cisterns overflowed, the wallpaper acquired cubic measurements, trains collided and people might well arrive somewhere before they started. It was hopeless, and my mentors hardly managed to get me to the most elementary fractions and decimals before I was seventeen, and that was it. Science we never touched in any shape or form.

   This rather shaky foundation was of course supplemented by extra-curricular activities. I knew my way about my father's library before I progressed to being sent there to prepare lessons for myself. My modest talent for drawing was fostered, after the age of fifteen, by a day a week at the county art school in Chelmsford and it was the Principal, Charles Baskett, who steered me into art history. The Girl Guides dragged me out of my daydreams and instilled efficiency in practical matters, encouraged private enterprise and inspired a sense of competition which had hitherto been conspicuously lacking. Parents and relations took great trouble in teaching us to play tennis in a reasonably competent if amateurish way. Although unsophisticated in the ways of the world we were probably rather more socially polished at seventeen than girls who emerged straight from boarding schools, and were endowed with quite a lot of thoroughly unjustified self-confidence.

Nine

VISITORS AND VISITING

The spare-rooms remind me of some of the guests who added such interest to our lives. The most frequent were our uncles and aunts, with whom we were on more informal terms than with most of the others. We never saw them before breakfast but at any other time of day the aunts would answer a tap on the door in a friendly manner and were prepared to chat while doing their hair, or accept help in fastening their dresses or jewellery. My senior aunt on my mother's side, and the least inhibited, had a lady's maid at home but our house, though apparently a large one, was so completely occupied that there was no room for extra servants and I do not remember that any ever came. Our head housemaid called the married couples or single ladies with early morning tea, accompanied by the thinnest of cut bread-and-butter. Breakfast in bed was unusual, really only justified by illness, and the maid would briskly draw a bath and announce when it was ready. This also served as a reconnaissance, because women did not like to be seen walking about the passages in their dressing-gowns. Just in case of an encounter, however, some of them wore lacy 'boudoir caps'.

It was considered good manners for guests to come down to breakfast about ten minutes, not more, after the gong had sounded, thus allowing time for their hosts to read letters and get the children started on the hot dishes. This was important because it was the children who did any waiting on the guests, although for the most part they helped themselves. I did, however, once stay in a house more old-fashioned than ours, and was appalled to find my elderly host and hostess waiting for me behind the huge silver kettle, and the magnificent row of hot dishes not yet started on. I had lurked in my bedroom so as not to be embarrassingly punctual.

I do not know what went on in the men's rooms but I suppose the butler or footman used to call them, take their shoes and clothes away for brushing, put studs ready in their evening-shirts and look after their sporting gear. All these services required substantial tips, or what seemed substantial in those days. The men's would run into pounds but except for a long stay of a week or more, ten shillings was probably usual for women to give to female servants. Single girls could get away with five shillings and as few of us worked and most were kept pretty short by their parents, in cash though not in kind, it was sometimes difficult, albeit absolutely essential, to reserve these sums. Porters and taxis might prove unexpectedly expensive, a loss at games in stakes reckoned in threepences would be disastrous, and a chauffeur instead of your host driving you to the station probably cost you your lunch on the train. One daughter of a particularly well-off family of our acquaintance was always ravenously hungry. On both sides the tipping was a perfectly well-understood convention, too much, too little or even, I suspect, nothing at all, being accepted with impeccable manners, whatever might be said in the servants' hall.

However pleasant the servants almost invariably were in the houses you stayed in, there was an uncomfortable feeling of having a cloud of witnesses about one, particularly where one had been previously known as a child. I felt outraged when my aunt's lady's maid, on saying goodbye to me, added 'tell Nanny I think you have improved wonderfully'. It was thought essential to have the proper equipment of matching brushes to be set out on the dressing-table. We were usually packed or unpacked for, and clothes were laid out on the bed before dinner. Should you wear without question what a strange housemaid had selected? Did she or you know best and if you felt she did not, would she be hurt if you substituted something else? Did your underwear come up to scratch and was there enough of it? You seldom stayed long enough to send things to the laundry and had no facilities for washing so much as a pair of stockings. These were of wool for some sporting occasions and took ages to dry, or the lisle threads for tennis might get green stains on them and silk ones laddered so easily. Many materials crushed fatally in spite of being packed with masses of tissue paper and, however you looked after some strenuous activity, you must never at the outset have a hair out of place, creases where you sat down or wrinkles in your stockings. The latter were particularly heinous. Maids had a kindly but devastating way of taking shoes away to be cleaned or clothes to be dried and ironed, but if they did not bring them back in time should you ring or keep everyone waiting? I never rang a bell for my own needs at home and would have done almost anything rather than ring one in a strange house.

It was probably even worse for young men, who had more at stake. Black or white tie in the evening? And if your shoes had not come up from being cleaned would your host think you effete if you came down to breakfast in slippers? There is little doubt that he would have. How much more damning than the solecisms of the drawing-room were those of the hunting field and the shooting party, under the baleful eye of perhaps your prospective father-in-law. Not only did men have to have the right clothes and equipment but these were expected to come from just a few right shops. Nevertheless, shooting parties came in many grades and on the whole did allow for considerably less domestic formality. Families from England would take lodges in Scotland in August and September, transport their whole households and invite friends to stay. These lodges were sometimes primitive, without electric light, adequate hot water or comfortable beds. Lunch was usually a picnic on a moor and guests, who were often asked for a fortnight or more, probably got to know their hosts more intimately than in home surroundings.

Our uncle and aunt, Stanley and Edith Gordon Clark, used to go each year to Wester Aberchalder in Inverness-shire and there, in the mid-twenties, you hardly went in a motor car unless it were to or from the station nearly twenty miles away. You walked to the shooting rendezvous and you walked all day. It was very much a man's world and you joined in the sport on condition of making yourself as useful and inconspicuous as possible. You must not expect anyone to carry things for you as the men already had enough, with their guns and cartridges, and sometimes you added to your burdens the care of a half-trained dog, still on a lead. You knew how to mark down birds and were rather like dogs yourselves – no bright colours, no loud voices or laughter, no lagging behind, no nonsense of any kind, but what sheer bliss it was. I wore a sober felt hat sometimes relieved by a jay's or pheasant's feather, or the highly-prized pin-feathers of a woodcock. My tweed coat and skirt were conservatively cut and would last for years, starting off when new for point-to-points and other country race-meetings, progressing from organized shoots with birds driven over butts, to rough days walking in line, until their chilliness made it apparent that they were well and truly worn out.

Flat candlesticks for taking up to bed

With these was assumed an 'Aertex' shirt of cellular cotton, and at least one jersey which could be shed at need into the haversack in which I carried the indispensable Burberry and my lunch if it was not the sort of day when the picnic was sent up on a pony. My stockings were woollen, in tweedy colours, my shoes hobnailed and as nearly waterproof as shoes can be. On informal days I carried an ash walking stick to beat out the bracken or, for driving days, a shooting stick on which I perched in somebody's butt.

In spite of all this strenuous sport, dinner in the evening remained formal. Somehow we bathed and changed into evening dress, my uncle made a seating plan every night for the party of about twelve and we ate a beautifully cooked and served dinner of never less than four courses. We grew adept at dismembering the many types of game which were the staple meat dish except for a mammoth joint of beef on Sundays. Sleepy as we all were, we then had an hour or so of home-made music with my aunt at the piano, parlour games or cards, before we picked up the flat candlesticks set out in a row in the hall, and retired to the idiosyncratically shaped and sparsely furnished bedrooms, to sleep like tops in the villianous beds.

This uncle and aunt, who had no children of their own, widened our horizons considerably. He was in a City timber business and active in the Merchant Taylors' Company. Their social net was more extensive than ours and from the family circle, the business one and their many charitable concerns they brought together a number of people. Looking back, I think they cannot all have been very compatible but they got on remarkably well under my aunt's amusing and impulsive hostess-ship. It was they who presented me at Court, or rather my aunt did, and my uncle, having attended levées in various capacities, accompanied us in a deputy-lieutenant's scarlet uniform. It was an exacting performance for the eighteen-year-old débutantes who had not been out much beforehand as adults in an adult world. First there were several fittings with a French dressmaker who

afterwards put in *The Times* your name, her name and what you
wore. My dress was white chiffon over a pink slip and as skirts were
then very short and waists very long, the belt area was round my hips
and I had great difficulty in not showing my knees. To my shoulders
was attached a separate silver lamé train which in due course was
frugally turned into another dress. With other girls I was made to
practise with a tablecloth how to curtesy without getting entangled in
a train, and to move off crabwise so as neither to turn my back on the
royal couple nor fall flat on the carpet. If you rose with your weight on
the wrong foot you could do just that. I carried a borrowed white
feather fan and at the back of my head, secured by a pearl bandeau
across my forehead, rose three ostrich feathers from which hung a
length of tulle. I had white kid gloves above the elbow and silver
brocade shoes with straps across the instep. My aunt, in a grey dress
with a lace train, wore some splendid diamonds of her own but had
also borrowed my mother's and a sister-in-law's. She was right, for it
was certainly an occasion on which to sparkle as much as possible, to
add your quota to the glittering scene in the splendid suite of
Buckingham Palace state apartments. George V and Queen Mary,
enthroned on a dais among the uniforms, brocades, medals and jewels
of an entourage which included some well-known public figures,
provided a climax I have never forgotten and they smiled at each
individual enough to make the curtseying and backward withdrawal
seem unalarming. This was one of the last Courts for which cars were
allowed to queue up in the Mall instead of waiting in the Palace
quadrangle. The milling East End crowds were good-naturedly
enjoying the show and their forthright comments were kindly, but
times were hard indeed for the urban poor in about 1927 and the
display seemed tactless.

All this was very different from the ambience of an aunt on my
father's side, Miss Susan Lawrence MP. We children knew her mostly
at my grandmother's house, Castlemans near Twyford, as an alarming person given to a kind of sophisticated teasing we were too young
to understand. With devastating cleverness she would rip through
your defences at Halma and after half a dozen moves your corner of
the board would be full of her men. By the time I was grown-up she
had been released – and release indeed was the word for it – from the
formality of a Victorian old lady's house with its strict routine upheld
by elderly servants, the carriage and pair the only means of access to
the railway station. Susan keeping the horses waiting, by returning

late from meetings in London, was a theme-song of my youth though my grandmother was sympathetic to the causes she espoused, and always had plenty of mauve, green and white Suffragette ribbon about. I knew her best when I was just grown-up and she was living alone in the Grosvenor Road, Millbank, in one of a row of balconied red brick and stucco houses which has now disappeared. Aunt Susan combined intense goodwill towards the human race in general, sympathy with the underdog, faithfulness and generosity towards friends and relations, with a total inability to get on comfortable terms with more than a very few intimates. I used to balance the advantage of having somewhere to stay in London against the sheer terror of her presence, but I did see that she really wanted the young to come, and my frequent acceptance of her hospitality was not wholly mercenary. Concealing as best I might the latest ravages of hunting or mixed hockey, which I sensed would be regarded as far from honourable scars, I would put on my very best evening dress at her request and sit either perfectly silent among her mainly Independent Labour Party friends or venture on orthodox conversational openings which were apt to be met by stares of incredulity. Her own ideas of dress were purely functional except when she made great efforts for family weddings, and I remember her at her handsome best in a lovely bright red straw hat which set off to perfection her rather swarthy complexion and large short-sighted dark eyes. The same view of dress characterized most of her friends and the younger, diminutive, Ellen Wilkinson MP was the only one I remember who obviously enjoyed clothes. I can see her now, red hair flaring about her head, sitting on the floor talking nineteen to the dozen about detective stories, the black and oyster satin panels of a wide skirt spread out around her, I am sure not wholly artlessly. One did not expect this sort of thing from Mrs Sydney Webb or Mrs Pethick-Lawrence.

Aunt Susan's was the only household of its kind that I knew at that time but I realize now that it must have been typical of her particular brand of intellectual, devoted to high thinking and simple living. The house was large for her so she had negotiated with a parliamentary colleague who made a way through from next door and had the use of what would have been her dining-room on the ground floor. This meant that her own was a small back room on the first floor and she furnished it with a plain deal table painted, probably by herself, in black with a red, green and gold dragon design. The chairs were simple kitchen ones. She could manage dinner parties of eight and

Lesley as presented at Court to King George V and Queen Mary in 1928. She wears a dress of white chiffon over a pale pink underslip and the diamanté bandeau holds in place, at the back of a shingled head, the obligatory feathers and tulle; the silver lamé train would have trailed three feet behind her. The long white gloves have been omitted for the studio photograph.

Pilgrims' Hall from the air. This photograph was taken in about 1965, but it shows that little has changed since the Second World War, except for the grassed-over main kitchen-garden and now dilapidated greenhouses.

frequently did, but in so confined a space there could be little waiting and dishes were placed on the table. The food was plain, plentiful and good, running to the then minimal three or four courses, starting with soup. As the ground floor was out of action everything had to be brought up from the basement by Miss Wordley, the taciturn general maid who had been there since anyone could remember. Aunt Susan thought it insulting to call a person by her christian name just because of her occupation but I used to reflect that although we never called our maids 'Miss' we would never have thought of working them quite so hard as Aunt Susan did Miss Wordley.

The big light room on the first floor, overlooking the river, was almost entirely lined with books and political publications, stuffed into and tumbling out of open shelves. Her desk was piled high with papers and she must have spent many hours a day working at it, smoking like a chimney. There was little space for pictures and except for a certain cult of contemporary art I do not think she had a real aesthetic sense; she probably felt no need to possess works of art or even decorative bric-à-brac. Threadbare rugs in drab colours left large areas of floor-boards uncovered and the numerous chairs used for her parties were old and battered. The bedroom I slept in at the top of the house was sparsely furnished, but delightfully painted pink, walls, ceiling and all, and the iron hospital bedstead with its worn sheets and blankets was no more uncomfortable than many others I met. At high tide the river used to twinkle on the ceiling, reminding one of Venice, Aunt Susan said, but it was just about the only thing which did. She was deliberately frugal, not from meanness but from a self-denial which enabled her to give generously to the causes she had at heart. She must have stifled all desire for the luxury in which she had been reared and which she still found in her relations' houses. However, though her normal conversation was of the lecturing kind, she did not lecture us about this and took in good part the ragging of bolder spirits among her nephews, who composed a Christmas parody for her, beginning:

'Hark the Daily Herald Sings,
Ruin to the best of Kings'

– and so on through several stanzas. Perhaps I should have been bolder myself but her extreme shyness engendered it in others, and robbed her of much in human relationships which her warm heart and noble qualities should have made hers by right.

An unmarried sister of my mother's lived in Steyning with a vaguely delicate and incompetent sister who could never have managed life by herself. By present-day standards my active aunt's existence would seem frustrated, but she lived it with zest, among a host of friends, and I do not think she ever felt sorry for herself, or others for her. When my grandmother died rather young she had to take over the household for a grim and forlorn widower and seven brothers and sisters of whom the youngest was a boy ten years old, my uncle Douglas. There was little money and she must have performed miracles of management but those days I did not know. I started going alone to stay with her when I was eleven years old and only the invalid Aunt Lily was still at home. The house was at one end of Steyning High Street, right on the road with a small front garden gravelled around two flower-beds in which bedding-out plants such as geraniums and lobelias were set out in season. Its front was that of a mid-Victorian villa in yellow and red brick but there was a much older core and, essential for what had been such a large family, a surprising number of rooms, mostly small and dark, on odd levels. The one I had was a slip opening out of my aunt's bedroom with space for little more than the bed. In the pleasant garden behind were three big old yew trees forming something like a summerhouse, and a small lawn on which we played at putting or bat-trap and ball, games suitable for a confined space. Beside the garden a lane ran straight up to the Round Hill, the nearest point in the range of South Downs culminating in Chanctonbury Ring. The downs were then completely uncultivated, with short springy turf grazed by sheep and rabbits, and a surprising variety of wild flowers new to an East Anglian child. Also, to one used to flat country it was thrilling to see the Weald spread out below in a chequerboard of different-coloured fields. The Ring was about the limit of our walks and on the way we would see the pinnacles of the unfinished Lancing School chapel and the mysterious round dewpond which was said never to dry up.

Springwells was intriguingly over-full with the excessive furniture and bric-à-brac of those who had lived in larger houses. It was probably in typically Victorian taste, with brass-mounted and rosewood furniture, water-colours in gilt frames, closely spaced on patterned wallpaper, many framed photographs and pretty Dresden china for which the sisters had acquired a taste at their finishing school. I do not think they remembered much of their German but one phrase at least stuck. My mother stroked the nose of a large carthorse and was nearly expelled becase its driver said 'Liebe mich auch, fraulein'. I immensely admired a brass writing-table set encrusted with large round polished black and white stones, and I was perhaps the only person who ever read the handsomely bound books laid out for ornament. My favourite was Aytoun's *Lays of the Scottish Cavaliers*, copiously illustrated with steel engravings. Some of what I afterwards knew to be period furniture had unfortunately been embellished with chip-carving, which was my grandfather's hobby.

The two excellent maids and gardener-handyman waited on us fairly thoroughly, and I do not think my aunt did any routine domestic work although she made jam and bottled fruit. I felt, however, much closer to real life than at home, and enjoyed being sent alone into the town to buy things for the household. Everyone knew everyone else in the High Street and many of the houses we went into were much smaller than any I had known before apart from labourers' cottages. Entertainments were simple, in little gardens at the back or in rough fields, where we played rounders. Parents took more part in this than the ones I knew at home and the fathers, who must have either worked in the neighbourhood or not worked at all, were available to organize us. The best days were when we went to Brighton which was the town for major shopping and for appointments with oculists and dentists. The aunts had a motorcar, still slightly unusual for such a household, and by 1920, when I first saw it, it was already fairly old. It was called a GWK, which stood for George Wood and Co, and was technically a two-seater; three people could in fact fit on the front seat, and a dickey folded into a well at the back, or when opened out overhung the rear, to take one more. A leather hood was fixed by straps at the front, but was seldom put up. The engine itself was just behind the front seat and what appeared to be an imposing bonnet covered only the occupants' feet. The car was painted fawn-colour and had a great deal of lovingly polished brasswork, including a large bulb horn.

Starting it was quite a drama and everyone but the driver stood well clear. Access to the front seat was on the passenger's side; the driver had no door, and had to lean over to operate the brass-handled brake on the outside. Aunt Emmie would lower an aspirin bottle on a string into the petrol tank and then pour a few drops from this into various parts of the engine. She then raised a flap in the running-board and cranked vigorously with the handle concealed below. The moment the engine fired she leaped into the driver's seat to wiggle the throttle and keep it going – the passenger could not get in first to do this for her because she could not then have climbed in. Few strangers could crank the car as it required a special knack rather than brute strength, and the days when I learned to do it were still far ahead. At about the third attempt, usually, the engine kept going steadily and we piled in, but we were not out of the wood yet. My aunt's method of getting into motion was to let in the clutch and gear, advance the throttle and take off the brake as nearly simultaneously as possible. When she was successful we took a great leap forwards but we often stalled and then everyone had to get out and the series of operations was repeated as before. We sped along gaily at up to forty miles an hour, my aunt driving in a very determined manner, firmly convinced that whatever other road-users did she was always in the right and, to do her justice, I think she usually was.

The GWK had a glorious death, or shall we say its final intimation of mortality, on Goodwood racecourse. It seized up on the run-in just when the horses were coming and the police lifted it off bodily with my aunt inside it. She would tell this story with a perfectly straight face and, in spite of a first-rate sense of humour in other respects, was not amused and did not expect others to be. In those days when you cherished things so much and kept them so long they became a kind of extension of your personality, and to laugh at them was to laugh at you.

Ten

THE BACK PREMISES

From the hush of the thickly carpeted front landing at Pilgrims' Hall, double doors led into a wide passage covered with highly polished dark green cork lino. On the left was a big table used for ironing or for sorting linen, lit by a window which overlooked a lead flat and the pantry skylight. In one wall of the well was an iron trapdoor to a flue which the sweep cleaned on his twice-yearly visits. These were among the few occasions of real disruption in the domestic routine as the chimneys had to be cooled and everything near them covered in dustsheets. The sweeps lived up to the sinister traditions of their calling, with faces as black as their clothes, the whites of their eyes standing out startlingly. They seldom removed their cloth caps, which had a metallic sheen like blackleaded grates. The maids must have given them food and drink, because the job lasted most of the day, but their hospitality lacked the cheerful matiness with which other visiting workmen were entertained. There could be no fraternization with such rough customers and no one ever seemed to know the sweeps off duty: their names and where they lived remained a mystery. They came in a low flat trap in which lay their circular brushes and the rods, joint upon joint, to be pushed up until the head emerged from the top of the chimney. The pony, of whatever colour he started, was as black as his master and so was the nosebag from which he ate his lunch. I am afraid we probably did not help him to get out the last oats by holding it up for him, as was customary with other guest-horses. There was a certain atmosphere of awe about the sweeps as if they really did come from nether regions. It was a relief when they went away, taking in sacks all the soot except a little left to deter slugs in the garden.

Beyond the big table two steps led down to the bathroom and lavatory used by the nursery and the maids. The latter had baths, on a rota system, usually in the middle of the afternoon or late at night, while we used the bath before breakfast and from about 6 to 7.30 pm. When the nursery was abandoned and some of us migrated to the front of the house the footman was allowed to come up in a dressing-gown to have a bath. Before that he had a hip-bath in the pantry and the butler of course had his at home in the lodge at the front gate. At the end of the passage, looking over the kitchen garden, was a housemaids' pantry performing the same function for this part of the house as the one on the front landing. Next it was a smallish square room, cosy because it was over the kitchen but characterless since no one ever settled down in it for long. It had a threadbare red carpet, an iron hospital bed and varnished furniture. For a time it was my bedroom but when the nursery was no longer needed as such I moved into that. Then Nanny had it as a bed-sitting-room and after she died it was occupied by a sewing maid. It evidently marked the end of the older part of the house, and in the passage which formed a T with the wide one the new wing must have been joined on. In the latter were a drying-cupboard, with slatted shelves and hot pipes, and the linen cupboard, unheated, in which the ample supplies of sheets were stored. Parents, the governess and visitors had unmended linen ones; children had cotton or linen ones which had been turned sides to middle as they became worn; the maids and footman had cotton. Outside the cupboards usually stood the big deep hampers, which needed two men to carry them and were sent away with the laundry each week.

In the middle the passage divided and on the right a staircase went up to the four maids' rooms. First came the cook's large sunny one looking out over the drive, and she used to have a fire to sit by in the afternoons, unless she was taking the opportunity of the kitchen being quiet to make some special pastry or ice a birthday cake. Next it was the head housemaid's smaller room, with the same view. In the two rooms at the back, looking over the stable yard and kitchen garden, the younger maids slept according to their departments, the kitchen-maid and scullerymaid in one and the two under-housemaids in the other. They were all furnished much the same, with fawn hair carpets; black iron bedsteads; dressing-table, washstand and wardrobe suites in brown grained wood, and floral-patterned toilet sets. There was no piped water in this part of the house so the maids washed mostly in their bedrooms, the slops being carried downstairs by one of the juniors, who must have been mainly occupied with waiting on her elders and betters. We occasionally went up to these rooms by invitation, to get a better view of what was happening in the stable yard, but normally they were out of bounds.

Six steps, covered with a red-bordered grey hair carpet, took off near the foot of the maids' staircase. They led to a lower level from which opened the doors of the day and night nurseries, which also communicated within and with a third room beyond them. The night nursery had a bow-window overlooking the drive and was furnished with a good light-oak suite which had perhaps come from my parents' or a spare-room in the previous house. Nanny's bed and ours, in contrast to the maids', were of white instead of black iron, with hair mattresses on interlacing wire springs. Nanny slept in this room with two girls and the baby, the nurserymaid with my brother in the inner one until he went to boarding school and was promoted in the holidays to a room in the front of the house. There were dark green cork lino floors, kept unpolished for fear of falls, and big rush mats by the washstands. The paint was white, the walls plain cream distemper, and the only concession to childhood lay in the Dutch tiles round the fireplaces, with children's games outlined in blue on a white ground.

The day nursery was where everything of interest happened. It was a large room with a canted bay-window overlooking the kitchen garden. In this recess stood a miniature table and chairs, much used for painting and other pursuits needing a good light. Nearby was the brown cloth-covered rocking horse, on a very solid stand, which was the centre of many games and a good deal of quarrelling. Beyond the window was an oilcloth-topped table where the baby's feeds were made up with the aid of a round spirit lamp. Along one wall stood a big Georgian mahogany wardrode, rather above its station perhaps but indestructible and destined to have a long post-nursery life in more dignified surroundings. On the far side of the room was a Dutch-tiled fireplace, shielded by the high wire guard which had moved with us and was secured to the wall by hooks. On one side of the blue and red Turkey hearthrug stood a low basket chair, almost totally monopolized by me, the book-worm, and on the other a cane-seated nursing chair on which Nanny sat to attend to the baby. In one corner a white cupboard contained biscuits, baby food and our china and cutlery; toys were kept in a stout oak one alongside. In the middle of the room a deal-topped table on turned reddish-varnished legs was covered by a green serge cloth which hung down far enough to make a cave underneath. There were six rush-seated chairs and a high chair for babies, a remarkable piece of furniture, solidly made in dark varnished wood. A tray was brought over the baby's head from the back for meals, firmly enclosing the occupant. At other times the whole chair could be hinged from the middle so that the baby sat as in a little cart. The underside of the base then became a tray, with coloured wooden balls strung on wires to play with. On the walls of the nursery hung a set of coloured prints by Cecil Aldin illustrating a whole day's hunting, from the meet to a highly convivial dinner. A big carved cuckoo-clock with hanging weights told the time for us, but the bird emerging noisily from his trapdoor on every hour sometimes frightened babies and had to be temporarily silenced.

Nursery meals were quite a battle. We seldom liked the food, picked at it and spilt it on the roughish chequered damask tablecloth. While we messed about, it got cold and even more unattractive, in spite of being put on hot-water plates of blue and white china on a hollow metal base. The dinner and tea service started as a clean shiny white with bright blue and gold rim but it became discoloured and crazed from much use, and the plated cutlery, monogrammed N for nursery, was not polished and much dulled with time. Far the best meal was tea, especially in winter when we made toast with the wire toasting-fork kept ready by the fire. Although it was an effort learning the conventions of the schoolroom and the dining-room, it was worth it for the food and the more inviting ways of serving it.

Our toys were numerous and mostly well made so that they lasted for years. We had an old musical box which you cranked up so that a comb passed over a prickly roller and played *The Bluebells of Scotland*, *Coming through the Rye* and *Annie Laurie* in a sweet tinkly way. It got stuck eventually and was put in the glory-hole under the front stairs, but when we were sheltering there from an air raid in 1940 a bomb landing particularly near started it off again and it has played ever since. There was a rather ordinary doll's house with a flat front painted to look like red brick; we played with it only by fits and starts, stimulated by gifts of miniature furniture and utensils. These, though bought new, were somewhat Victorian in style. My brother had a good green clockwork engine and a set of rails, I a rather tinnier engine with lines of a wider gauge, which perhaps reduced quarrelling as they were not interchangeable. We had quantities of beautifully made lead toy soldiers accompanied, in my brother's case, by a gun,

gun-carriage and team, which took apart, and in mine by a field
ambulance of similar make. As it was wartime we were very militarily
minded when small, and our jerseys were adorned with regimental
buttons, badges and scarlet staff gorget tabs given us by our uncles or
the maids' young men. Anything went, whether from a private or a
full colonel, but the most handsome item was a pair of Indian Cavalry
chain-mail epaulettes belonging to my brother, who generously used
to let me wear one sometimes. The toy we used the most, and which
came into games with trains and soldiers as well, was a box of German
bricks, made of stone or stone composition, red, blue-grey and white.
On the lid was a picture of what I now know to have been a
Romanesque church façade, but we were never interested in the
makers' examples in anything, preferring 'something out our own
heads', as we called it. I had a large family of teddy bears and one doll,
for which I made endless clothes out of the scraps left over from
grown-up dress-making. As the 'Bing Boys', these characters figured
on the front page of a magazine I produced when I was twelve,
plagiarized no doubt from the strip series in the children's papers *Puck*
and *Rainbow*, but with more original contributions, competitions and
the like inside. My magazine only ran for eleven copies and then
ceased 'for lack of readers'. Perhaps at one penny it was too expensive
for my public.

For out of doors, my brother had a little trolley, worked with a
transverse handle and called 'the Racer', and I had a doll's pram, the
exact replica of our full-sized ones. We seldom played games round
the table by ourselves but with grown-ups we would settle down to
Snap, Animal Grab, Old Maid or Donkey, or the Race Game with its
delightful pictorial board and set of lead horses. It had dice, however,
and Nanny would not allow these on Sundays, any more than she
would the ordinary playing cards. Plain sewing was also barred on
Sundays but not knitting and cross-stitch. No books were forbidden
but some were only brought out then, such as Nanny's own copies of
The Wide Wide World, *Bruce Heriot's Trial*, *The Rosary* and *Eric or Little
by Little*. These, supplemented by the novels which appeared in
instalments in the maids' *Daily Mirror*, provided me with the romance
and sentiment I adored. I must, however, have read the crime pages as
well because odd details of famous murders still come back to me.

Just outside the nursery door the back stairs descended to the
flagged and tiled passages of the kitchen area. People were always
running up and down these stairs, usually carrying things, and the

only quiet time of day here was in the middle of the afternoon and during staff mealtimes. Along the flagged corridor from the stairs to the pantry was a row of filled coal-scuttles or the zinc liners for the wooden ones with sloping lids which were in most of the rooms, and many of these had to be brought upstairs. Then in the morning the housemaids would be carrying the tin-lined white wooden boxes with sloping sides, used for cleaning grates and laying fires. Each had a tray on top containing brushes, black-lead powder for ironwork and special cloth gloves kept for the job. The lower part would hold newspaper and kindling or cinders and ashes cleared from the grate. The gardeners were supposed to keep up the supply of dry kindling and the footman and bootboy to keep scuttles filled with coal of suitable sizes for starting and replenishing the fires. On the rare occasions, when staying away or when ill in bed, that one watched a housemaid doing the fire, one admired the skill with which the iron was blackleaded and polished, the grate layered with newspaper, sticks and small coals, and the whole thing neatly finished off by a flat sheet of paper behind the bars.

In the space under the stairs was the storeroom with grey-painted shelves and cupboards all round and a red-tiled floor. My mother, in consultation with the butler, cook and head-housemaid, would order from the Army and Navy Stores six months' supplies of yellow bar soap for rough scrubbing, soft soap like green jelly for washing up, floor polish, furniture polish, metal polish, boot polish, marmalade in large stoneware jars, brushes and broom-heads. Jam for the family was ordered seasonally from the Tiptree factory and ordinary groceries from the local town. These things were dispensed from the storeroom only by, or by permission of, my mother or the cook, although the key lay on the chimneypiece for all to see. Here also were numerous jars of home-made jam, and bottles of gooseberries, plums, raspberries and blackcurrants prepared in season and used for dishes of stewed fruit and Sunday tarts throughout the year. Relegated unused china and glassware, and the last pathetic remnants of much-loved sets which no one had the heart to throw away, were stored here, and there were always a few copies of the fascinating Army and Navy catalogues, bound in red cloth: these were a major source of general knowledge with their copious illustrations of familiar and unfamiliar objects, from games equipment to medical appliances, with the prices of everything and lovely colour plates of china.

Red-tiled passages led to the back door and the so-called nursery door where, in our childhood, the prams stood. On one side of it was a larder with slate shelves, hooks for game, and a huge zinc-lined icebox, filled with a great slab which used to be brought in sacking from the fishmonger's. On this the fish would be laid, but other food stood out on the shelves, cooled by the north and east breezes which came in through the pierced metal of the flyproof windows. On the other side, under the night nursery and so having a similar bow-window, was the dairy, also fitted with wide slate shelves. The head-gardener's sister, Nellie Roscoe, was in charge here, an admirable Lancashire woman who had been on a dairying course at the Chelmsford agricultural institute. She wore the black cloth-topped clogs of her native land to keep out the cold and wet from the floor, which was scrupulously sluiced down. In the afternoon the cowman brought in pails of milk and helped her use the separator, which started up with a characteristic whine punctually every day at 4 pm. Its innumerable aluminium parts were scalded immediately after use, the foaming skimmed milk taken away for the pigs, and the cream put aside for butter, which was made twice a week. The churn was of metal-banded wood, and one of the men used to turn it until Nellie heard the thumps which indicated that the butter was coming, when she took over herself. She rolled it to get out surplus moisture, salted it, and with grooved wooden 'hands' divided it into pound and half-pound slabs and little round pats for the dining-room butter dishes. Sometimes she flattened these pats by stamping them with a wooden die, leaving the impression of an oak or maple leaf. If the separator went wrong the milk was poured into big shallow enamel pans, about a yard across, and she skimmed the cream off with a pierced metal saucer. When the old farm buildings were pulled down, however, the dairy became a second larder and all this interesting activity was removed from the house to the new farmstead. The herd was increased and we started supplying our neighbours with dairy produce.

A door out of the same passage opened into the servants' hall, a big room under the nursery with the same canted bay, in which stood an octagonal table with an aspidistra on it. On wet days this was put on the path outside to have a wash and freshening-up. In the middle of the room was a dining table with several leaves, and all the staff meals were eaten here, Nanny and the nurserymaid joining the others for supper at 8.45 after we had gone to bed. The cheerful sounds of conversation and laughter, and the clatter of plates and cutlery would be wafted up to us. There were armchairs round the fireplace and over it a sepia engraving of Landseer's 'Monarch of the Glen' in a wide maple frame with gilt slip. As a great treat we were sometimes invited to play whist with the maids after tea. This was a serious matter because some of them were very good at it and used to win prizes at whist drives in the village club. We eschewed the frivolity with which we approached card games in the front of the house, and were careful to do nothing to forfeit this valued privilege. The half-dozen flat-irons used for all the domestic ironing were ranged along the passage outside, up to near the kitchen door where a slightly shorter one led to the back door, outside which was a lavatory for the menservants. This back door was the one in most constant use, the route for the indoor staff, the tradesmen and for gardeners bringing in produce. Neither this nor the nursery door were ever locked during the day, there being far too many people about for any danger of intruders.

The junction of the new wing with the old house evidently came near the kitchen door, where there was a transition from tiled to stone-flagged floors. The kitchen was in the old part, a lofty room sited over the cellar which contained the boiler for the hot-water system and piles of anthracite to fuel it. The younger gardeners took it in turns, week by week, to stoke it three times a day, and although they usually entered by an outside door there was an inner one opening on to the passage beside the kitchen. A space behind this door allowed for a little courtship of the maids, unobserved or at least ignored by the cook and, in one case at least, ripening to a long and happy marriage. As you entered the kitchen, having made sure the cook would not object, you had on your right, occupying almost all of the wall, a huge black Eagle range. It had a central grate, stoked from the top through a round trap, and two ovens on each side. They were of different temperatures, for different purposes, but it took much skill and experience to get and keep them to the required heat. Everything about the stove was heavily made of iron, always extremely hot, and there was much clatter in the opening and shutting of oven doors, shooting coal in at the top and replacing the cover over the trap. The state of the fire could be seen through the bars in the centre and this was the one place where toast could be made, whatever else was going on. I cannot think how we had as much toast as we did, although there never seemed to be quite enough. The top of the range was just one big hot plate and on part of it, ready to be moved over for boiling up, stood an iron kettle and an iron saucepan for stock, both of heroic size. Above was a shelf for heating plates and dishes, although the cooler ovens often had to be used for this too.

On the left of the door was a long serving slab and a hatch through which the pantry staff collected and returned the dishes for meals. Nearby stood a marbled brown tin flour bin, round and about four feet high, kept full and with a shovel inside. Along the remaining walls were grey-painted cupboards for stores, pie-dishes, crockery and miscellaneous equipment. The cooking was mostly done in copper saucepans, very numerous because some had to go away from time to time to be tinned inside. The maids used to clean them with vinegar and very fine silver sand, of which I used to beg some for the bottom of my birdcage. There were copper moulds too, for jellies, mousses, blancmanges and meat loaves, and all these beautifully burnished objects, ranged on the higher shelves, made the kitchen bright. In the middle was an enormously solid table of plain wood, scrubbed to whiteness, and another smaller one stood in the window for more delicate tasks. Fly-papers hung from the top light, catching a surprising number of flies on their sticky surfaces; two or three breakneck mousetraps on the floor caught their quota of victims even though there was a kitchen cat.

A scullery opened out of the kitchen, its two wide shallow sinks under the window having wooden plate-racks on one side. It was not until I washed up here myself, in the 1939 war, that I realized how inconvenient the equipment was. Possibly the sinks had not been too low in the days when most people were shorter, but the width across them to the taps was singularly ill-adapted to any human frame. Partly no doubt because of this, the breakages were enormous, and huge orders for replacements would go off periodically to Goode's china shop. Washing soda was used freely to defeat the grease and was very hard on gilding and colour, while the soft soap made everything appallingly slippery. Food was usually delivered to the cook in a fairly rough state. Vegetables came in with earth and waste matter on them and all birds were plucked and drawn in the scullery, eggs sometimes being extracted from inside the chickens. Hares and rabbits were skinned and gutted, and large codfish with staring eyes had to have their heads cut off. The scullery was no place for the squeamish. No wonder cooks had to be approached with care; not only did they have to produce dining-room meals, servants' hall meals, nursery ones and schoolroom trays, but everything had to be done on time. They were often training their staff, because kitchenmaids would soon learn enough to go out as cooks themselves, and it is not really surprising that the daughters of the house had no chance to learn to cook. Among the great sharp knives and heavy cast-iron appliances, which could cut, burn and mince unpractised fingers, non-combatants were better out of the ring, and the only things I ever 'helped' with were grinding coffee in the iron mill with a little drawer under it, and rubbing things through sieves. Of course everyone was invited in to stir the Christmas puddings in November and make a wish.

In the long dark passage where the coal-scuttles were ranged, hung the red and blue woolly sausage which was the handle of the rope for the big bell on top of the house. In our early days the footman used to ring it for staff lunch at 1.30 but if he pulled too hard, as he fairly often did, the bell went over the bar. The gardeners then had to go up on the roof with ladders to swing it back, a cause of interdepartmental friction which it was best to avoid. A shrill electric bell was later used instead and the big bell only heard when my mother rang in the New Year. I do not think anything ever seriously disturbed the basic solidarity of the employed vis-à-vis the employer but there were traditional mild feuds, probably the same in all such houses, between stable and garden, garden and kitchen, kitchen and pantry, kitchen and nursery, nursery and schoolroom. One grew up in a vague awareness of these and cagily regulated one's doings so as not to be caught between two fires.

A swing door, glass-paned at the top to see through, but solid enough to stand being habitually kicked open, was part of the anti-cooking-smell precautions and divided the kitchen from the pantry quarters. Through this the trays were carried to and from the service door of the dining-room which opened into a small dark lobby. Here a long low cupboard held little-used big dishes, its top providing a service slab. Another cupboard held the water-jugs, vases and bowls which my mother needed for doing the flowers, and there were doors through to the front hall and the telephone lobby, where the gong was sounded. A flight of steps, guarded by a gate, led to the well-stocked cobwebby wine-cellar, and on the wall opposite the pantry door were the bell indicators. A bell from a downstairs room would be answered by the butler or footman but if it was from a bedroom or the schoolroom the man would give a pre-arranged number of rings on a bell heard upstairs by the maids. My parents, the governess or visitors would always ring rather than go and ask for something, unless they sent a child with a message, this not being regarded as an infringement of staff privacy.

The pantry door was normally kept shut to confine the smell of tobacco, the considerable consumption of which was the basis for our collections of cigarette cards. These were usually about $1\frac{1}{2}$ by $2\frac{1}{2}$ inches, with a beautifully printed picture on one side and explanatory text on the other. They were in series but it was difficult to get a whole set as the packets did not indicate which card would be inside. There were Uniforms of the British Army, Captain Scott's Expedition, Napoleon's Campaigns, Famous Paintings and sometimes, with Turkish cigarettes, a miniature carpet for the doll's house. At the window end of the pantry was a sink in which stood a wooden bowl so that silver could be washed without getting scratched. The early morning and afternoon tea-sets, glasses and dessert plates were washed here, but anything for the main courses or needing to be heated went to the kitchen. There was a fire in one corner with a good accurate clock on the mantelshelf, and solid cupboards, chests and brushing surfaces surrounded the room. These were continued into the small bedroom in which the footman slept. His livery was a dark green tailcoat with gilt crested buttons, black dress trousers, a waistcoat with narrow black, yellow and white horizontal stripes, a butterfly collar and white bow tie. In the pantry, however, he and the butler were usually in shirt sleeves and green baize aprons. A series of houseboys, for a year or so on first leaving school, did various jobs in the background, cleaned all but my parents' shoes, and polished the knives, in a little outside room in the stable range. Clamped to a bench was a circular appliance into which emery powder was poured out of a tin with the Duke of Wellington's head on it. A few knives at a time were inserted into leather-lined sockets and got polished when a handle was turned. The best quality dining-room knives were, however, cleaned individually on a board. None were made of stainless steel and the system of cleaning, while defeating rust, wore them to an extreme sharpness, thinness and indeed shortness. They had to be handled with care, and cut fingers, tied up with the clean old rags which were always available, were to be expected in children and the younger maids.

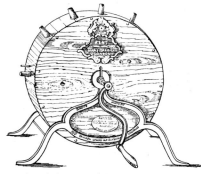

Knife-polishing machine

The pantry staff's day started with my father's call at 6.30 and they would bring down any clothes needing attention. They opened up the heavy wooden internal shutters with which all the principal rooms were equipped, brought in our breakfast, had their own and then saw him off to the station at 8.30. Washing up and valeting work probably took till 11, when with the rest of the staff they adjourned to the servants' hall for bread and cheese. From then until they started luncheon preparations they cleaned silver, a task to which a quite extraordinary amount of time and skill was devoted. Mostly they used Goddard's pink plate powder, damped with ammonia in an old saucer. It was left on for a few moments, then polished off with a chamois leather or, for engraved or heavily embossed pieces, a soft brush. Everything that had been cleaned was washed in hot soapy water and put away in drawers and cupboards to exclude the air, which tarnished silver within a few days. There was a strict rotation for everyday things, and those only used for special occasions were put away in tissue paper or green baize bags. Such was the pretty little brandy saucepan on its spirit lamp, which was only used for the Christmas plum pudding, and only by my father after the butler singed his eyebrows off with it. Every so often the table silver was cleaned with rouge instead of plate powder, to remove scratches and impart a deep, almost blackish, shine. Quite a lot of the surface silver must have been removed by the men's hard rubbing with strong fingers, and on some pieces the crests and engravings had been almost worn away. Care of silver was the special craft of good butlers and one which a footman would want to learn from him; they kept the plate in marvellous condition, could do such maintenance jobs as pressing out minor dents, and saw that anything needing mending went off to the silversmiths, in our case Tessiers of Bond Street.

It has always seemed odd to me that silver went on being used for so long for many purposes for which it was highly unsuitable and made a great deal of work. Salvers, for handing things, were always getting scratched, and much of the laborious rougeing was devoted to them. Sauceboats allowed their contents to get cold very quickly, as did silver teapots, hot-water jugs and coffee pots. Worst of all were the entrée dishes into which cooked food had to be transferred, since they could not themselves be put in the oven or on the top of the stove. Ceramic vessels which would both stand heat and look elegant enough beside the rest of the equipment – the shining cutlery, delicate engraved glassware and immaculate white damask – had probably not been invented.

Peace descended on the pantry in the early afternoon, with one of the men sitting by the fireplace in an armchair, only occasionally disturbed by the front-doorbell or by my mother needing to be seen off somewhere in the car or carriage. Activity set in again for tea, the return of my father from the station at 6.30, dinner and the shutting up of the house for the night. We come out into the front hall from the pantry lobby and our tour of the house is complete.

Eleven

OUR COUNTRYSIDE

We were only about twenty miles from London, half an hour's journey by the best trains from Brentwood to Liverpool Street, but the district was still as rural as those much further away. There had been a certain amount of development around the railway station, which was about three-quarters of a mile downhill from the town, and the old grammar school had recently been expanded into a large complex of new brick buildings. Near it, just south of the High Street, the hollow trunk of an ancient oak tree marked the place where the local martyr, William Hunter, was burnt at the stake in the days of Bloody Mary, but he was also commemorated more permanently by a brick and stone obelisk at the nearby crossroads. There were three good brick Georgian houses in the High Street, two occupied by doctors and the third by a solicitor who was the brother of one of them. The half-timbered Mitre House and Priory testified to something earlier and the White Hart Inn still kept its galleried rear premises in which coaches had been loaded. Except as a staging post, however, Brentwood had never been of any consequence, the small priory chapel visited by pilgrims on their way to Canterbury being its only claim to fame. The church was a nineteenth-century one and the big neighbouring parishes of South Weald and Shenfield had in early times been much more important. There was a flourishing Roman Catholic community and a large Ursuline convent, outside which we occasionally saw a Belgian royal princess who, owing to the war, was being educated there. Little is now left of any older buildings of distinction, the considerable public spirit of the inhabitants having been devoted to social improvement rather than conservation. Perhaps the Victorian accretions such as Wilson's corner shop with its clock will fare better.

For about half a mile northwards from the station towards home we passed terraces of small brick and stucco houses always in those days called villas, probably minor developments by local builders who had named them after distant places such as Rotorua, which was in a New Zealand group. Another terrace had Scottish names. We never knew anyone who lived in them and the homes of the High Street shopkeepers – the ironmonger, the fishmonger, the drapers and the stationer – were outside our experience. I doubt whether at that date the town and villages fraternized much on any social level, most people going only as far as they could walk.

Once past the Robin Hood Inn on the Ongar road, and some villas around it, you saw nothing but fields and small patches of poor woodland until you came to a red and yellow brick Victorian house close to the road. An elderly couple living there were the first people we knew who had a wireless; in the early 1920s we were invited in to hear Children's Hour and birthday greetings, which Mr Barrett got rather faintly by manipulating what he called a 'cat's whisker' in his crystal set. Then came the Rose and Crown, a small white inn which looked very old, set back just before a crossroads. Here minor roads led to South Weald on the left and Pilgrims' Hatch on the right, the former being preferred as a nursery or schoolroom walk. It had more interesting fauna and flora and no houses from which people might emerge and delay us with exasperating grown-up talk. They would please Nanny by admiring the current baby, familiarity with whom had bred in the older children a certain healthy cynicism; or even worse, they might praise our appearance.

There were perhaps twenty or thirty houses in Pilgrims' Hatch, and the baker's wife, a voluble and lively character, often emerged from hers when she saw us coming. Her husband must have become too prosperous for her to work in the shop and she probably had a maid, so had plenty of time for talk, and talk she certainly did. She was one of the housewives to whom the Women's Institute, formed in the 1920s, brought wide new interests and outlets for creative activity. She took to basket-making in raffia and wicker, glove-making, jam-making, wine and pickle brewing, and used to load us with gifts, somewhat embarrassing by reason of her own sweet tooth and the flamboyance of her taste. Her last present to me was for my wedding in 1944, a shawl crocheted in red, white and blue. The baker never said much but his presence was impressive, a gold watchchain looped across the waistcoat of his smart brown suit and his large moustache having its ends waxed to sharp points. Beyond the bakery was another substantial house belonging to Mr Hammond, one of the most important land-owners in the district and head of the considerable nonconformist congregation which met in a chapel next to his house. He had extensive orchards and fields cropped for market, much of the work being done by gangs of women roughly dressed in drab tattered clothes with broken boots and sometimes men's cloth caps. I think of them as a permanent feature but they must have come from outside for seasonal work as they did not live in any of the cottages we knew. These were occupied by the employees of establishments like ours, or craftsmen and farm labourers. They were mostly of clapboard construction with slate roofs, some neatly painted white with green doors and window-frames but many, probably the older ones, tarred black.

Further along the main road, on your right, was the village pond. It was roughly circular, about ten yards across and sloping back to no great depth from its gravelled edge on the road. Although not obviously fed by any running water it never completely dried up and was not stagnant, perhaps because it was stirred up so much. Carts were driven right into the middle of it to be washed down, passing horses and cattle drank from it and ducks were permanently in residence. Opposite was the Black Horse, a larger and probably more frequented inn than the humble little Rose and Crown. Unfortunately its Georgian stucco was stripped off at some later date and some half-timbering exposed or even fabricated in some brewer's misguided attempt to make it look Tudor, but it always had a nice pictorial sign. These were then comparatively rare, our local public houses usually having only lettered boards. We never saw inside any of them and so strong was the taboo that I would not go into the Black Horse or the Rose and Crown now, although there is no one left to be shocked. We were not even allowed in on the frequent wartime flag-days which were a great feature of my childhood and gave us the entrée to many farms and cottages. Although the average labourer must have been on a very small weekly wage the wives rarely refused us a penny or two and sometimes produced a sixpence from a tin on the chimneypiece or some other hiding place.

The typical cottage, usually semi-detached, had a front room into which the front door opened directly, a kitchen beyond it and two rooms above, reached by a stair which was little better than a ladder. There was usually a rear extension which housed a copper and mangle. The former was a bowl about two feet across embedded in brick or concrete with a fireplace underneath and it was used for laundering or for any demand for hot water beyond the capacity of kettles on the kitchen stove. Coppers were to be found in farm buildings as well for brewing up pigfood and you dipped into them with a basin attached to a wooden handle. The mangle was a strong iron contraption with rollers which wrung the water out of the bigger articles before they were hung out to dry on the line in the back garden. The work must have been extremely heavy for women and took up most of Monday, so this was not a day on which to call, nor was Friday, the usual shopping day. Otherwise we generally found the wives at home and they often asked us in.

You usually went in by the back door through the kitchen, the front one being permanently sealed against draughts, at least in winter. The front rooms, pleasant though rather dark by our standards, were full of fascinating objects crowded together. Chairs and settees were likely to be plush-upholstered with crocheted antimacassars but there might be a comfortable rush or cane-seated rocking-chair. Ferns stood in brass bowls and often a glazed cupboard contained china ornaments, souvenirs from holidays and the like, which might now be regarded as collectors' pieces. On the walls would be brightly coloured plates suspended by wires, or perhaps a text or two in pokerwork – burnt in brown on a pale wood background. Usually a pair of framed professional photographs would show our hostess and her husband at the time of their wedding, perhaps posed against plaster balustrades or simulated curtains such as we saw in the Brentwood photographer's studio. Occasionally we were shown treasures such as the little gilded tin box of comforts which was Queen Mary's gift to the soldiers in the trenches one year, and had been sent home with the belongings of a son who had been killed. We never went upstairs and the invalids whom we were required rather unwillingly to visit had their beds in the front room. Such was poor Harold who went in and out of hospital with the tuberculous hip which was then a common complaint. Main water from taps was available only in the kitchen or scullery and there were no bathrooms or indoor lavatories. Earth closets were usual and, I suspect, contributed greatly to the fertility of cottage gardens. One tenant of ours, a particularly skilful jobbing gardener, was enraged when my father insisted on installing water sanitation. Many of the gardens were indeed admirable, with roses, madonna lillies, crowns imperial, red-hot pokers, hollyhocks, bright annuals in front of the house, and vegetables grown at the back or in allotments elsewhere.

After the Black Horse a filthy lane led through a farmyard to a post office which must have been one of the smallest and dirtiest in all England. Its shop window was in the side of an old weather-boarded house which at some long-ago period of prosperity had acquired a grand red brick Georgian front, as had a number of farmhouses in the neighbourhood. Prosperity had, however, ebbed away and the revenue from the little shop was probably a considerable help to the farm during the agricultural depression of our youth. Having negotiated ankle-deep muck or deep baked ruts according to season, you pushed open the door and waited for the postmistress to emerge on hearing the tinkle of the bell. She was very old and so small that a child did not have to grow more than a few inches to be able to gaze with fascinated horror on the grime which encrusted the top of her venerable head. I still shudder at the idea of licking stamps which she pushed across the cluttered counter, but no one seemed to mind then and she did quite a trade, though not with us, in the villainous-looking sweets she packed into paper cornets. There were bootlace-like strings of liquorice, sugary balls in suspiciously brilliant pinks, greens and yellows, bars of unwrapped chocolate and striped peppermints. She also sold duck eggs, presumably from the birds on the village pond. The post office remained long after her day but has now been moved into a smart new shop on the road. The pond was filled in many years ago and built over, forming the nucleus of what is now a small shopping centre for the greatly increased population of the building development. Few wooden cottages remain in anything like their original state, but changes have been rapid and there must be people who can remember bringing up families in them so laboriously.

The first modern houses I remember being built in Pilgrims' Hatch were a group put up by the local council on the corner opposite the Rose and Crown. They were an enormous improvement on all cottages except those few special ones built by land-owners for senior staff such as butlers, chauffeurs, head-gardeners and gamekeepers. I recall the astonishment with which it was learnt that their rent would be twelve shillings and sixpence a week compared to the customary four shillings or half-a-crown. Two people who moved into them straight away were those pillars of society the policeman and the district nurse. The latter visited chronic cases or helped in emergencies but was primarily the village midwife, nearly all births taking place at home, often without a doctor. The service was paid for partly by subscription to a local association of which my mother was honorary secretary for many years. Echoes only reached me long afterwards of the stupendous row with which it had started, an older régime objecting to the nurse assisting at illegitimate births. My father, as chairman of the parish council, was obliged to take positive action on the side of tolerance, and a new committee was formed. A memorable incident was a Trollopeian member of the old guard driving off in her pony cart exclaiming 'Hoity-toity' after remonstrating with my mother; I believe we were never spoken to again from that quarter. My mother was a good choice, being discreet to the point of obscurantism: no one would ever know from her who was a bastard and who was not, or who had jumped the gun. The nurse used to come to the house frequently to report and put in for supplies, starting with a bicycle but graduating to an Austin Seven in which she drove around in her blue uniform with her black bag.

A small corrugated-iron building, painted rust-red, stood at the next crossroads. The 'tin hut' had been put up by the nonconformists but was let for all kinds of activities and, apart from the school, was for a long time the only place for meetings, jumble sales and other functions. The Boy Scouts used it as did the Girl Guides to which my sisters and I belonged. It was perhaps twenty-four feet by twelve, heated by a cylindrical cast-iron 'Tortoise' coke stove. This roasted anyone near it but did little for the general temperature; indeed it did not need to after the room had been full for an hour or so, especially if the oil lamps were lit. The tin hut was superseded by the foundation of a village club in a wooden hut bought from surplus army stores after the war. Gradually the rough ground around this was turned into tennis courts, the Women's Institute flourished, dances and whist drives became popular and the multifarious demands of the second world war made it the centre of village life. Pebble-dashed and still looking solid after more than half a century, at a hundred pounds it was a good bargain.

From here the 'straight mile' led past our own fields and drive gates on the left and some of the Hammond orchards on the right, with only a few houses to break the green and leafy aspect. Although it was the main road to Ongar it carried little traffic and the schoolchildren straggled over it, playing their games on the metalled surface. A pony, with no guiding hand on the rein, used weekly to bring home in perfect safety the trap containing a stout neighbour who always drank too much at Romford market. At the end was the church, out of sight to the left, with the school on the right. Here too was Millfield, a house about the same size as ours, with a similar establishment and four children who were our near contemporaries. My younger sister married the elder son and a daughter shared lessons with us. There were three other comparable households which supported our church and with which we were always in close touch. Dytchleys, on a road to South Weald, was the home of an old lady with three middle-aged spinster daughters. They were immensely active in parish good works but also fond of sport, kept ponies and horses, gave tennis parties and had innumerable relations to stay. Close to them was an equally large house called Gilstead Hall, occupied by a couple without children who nevertheless always had a great deal going on and used to invite us to fish in their pond. At Coxtie Green, also on the road to South Weald, was Oakhurst, where there lived for some years a lively family slightly younger than ours. They were allowed to do all sorts of things forbidden to us and, with no fears about fire, had at Christmas parties a huge snapdragon – a dish of raisins flaming with brandy from which you grabbed blisteringly hot threepenny bits. During most of my youth these families and ours were the leaders of the community in that small radius, employing and providing cottages for many people. As our church was then a chapel-of-ease to South Weald with a resident curate instead of a vicar, there was probably less leadership from the clergyman than was usual in the country, and much depended on the laity.

For a long time when I was young the road past our house was the only metalled one nearby but even so it was hardly built for speed. Every now and again a gang of men with cauldrons of boiling tar would appear, accompanied by a beautiful steam-roller adorned with gleaming brass. It chugged backwards and forwards rolling gravel and stone chippings into liquid tar and causing considerable inconvenience. The tar dried slowly, especially in hot weather, and there was much grumbling when it stuck to our shoes and clothes and pram-wheels. The steam-roller was apt to upset horses, probably those whose owners had not prudently turned them out in fields alongside roads where they would get used to such monsters. Some steeds, however, were incorrigible and my mother's little chestnut used to whip round in panic even at ordinary motor cars. He was called Discount because he had been bought cheap, and one can guess why, by his previous owner Field Marshal Sir Evelyn Wood, a VC of the Indian Mutiny, who used to hunt with the Essex packs. Discount was an excellent hunter, and evidently his owners thought his idiosyncrasies worth putting up with.

The minor untarred roads needed much day-to-day upkeep. They had wide grass verges in which every few yards was a small channel or 'grip' draining surface water into a big ditch which, usually combined with a hedge, was a field boundary. A permanent roadman, the same for many years, kept the grips clear and straight-sided, made up the potholes from heaps of stones and gravel at the roadside and removed obstructions from the ditches. He did not, however, cut the long grass and the verges were rich in wild flowers which varied according to our patchy soil. Mostly this was a stiff clay which at lower levels had blue veins in it, but there were sandy areas where toadflax and harebells grew. The hedges – a mixture of hawthorn, blackthorn, holly, elder, and saplings of various kinds, strengthened by brambles, wild rose-bushes, ivy, old man's beard and honeysuckle – were interspersed with big trees, some very fine. In this area of poor farming you seldom saw any good cut-and-laid fences but the rough bushes were wonderful for birds' nests and the ditches were full of life. In dry weather field-mice and shrews ran along the grips and were some-times to be spotted emerging on the road. Rustlings and the occasional squeal betrayed the presence of stoats, rats, rabbits or a domestic cat gone wild and there was always the hope of seeing something rarer. In fact I never remember doing so, foxes and badgers keeping well hidden and hedgehogs and moles being seen only as pathetic little corpses having come to grief on the road. They would be awarded a funeral if there was time.

In dry weather our walks were not limited to the roads. There were numerous footpaths because it was, and had probably been for a long time, a fairly populous district. Labourers went from the village to work at farms far from the road, or families walked from isolated cottages to the centres of local life – church, school, forge, shop or public house. So plentiful were the established paths that there was little temptation to trespass on private property which, however well you knew the owner, was strictly respected. Whatever was sown in a field over the line of a path was quickly trampled out by daily passers-by and the exact track was retained year after year. They were rarely bridlepaths and, to keep out any but foot-passengers, rather awkward stiles combined with plank bridges had to be negotiated at boundaries. They were roughly made but lasted a long time and a new plank or rail was a matter for comment. A lady usually needed help in getting over and a gentleman would stand in a charming and unforgettable attitude on the far side, holding out his hand but averting his eyes for fear he should inadvertently catch a glimpse of knicker beneath the skirt. It was delightful, especially when you were still rather small, to tread the narrow path in single file through a field of standing hay or tall wheat and oats. I suspect there were many more weeds than would be allowed today and the hay was of very mixed grasses, interspersed with clover and far too many buttercups. Poppies, marguerite daisies, tansy, scarlet pimpernel, white bindweed and pink convolvulus rioted amid the corn.

It was a countryside of small enclosed fields with much hedgerow timber and few open spaces. One which delighted us when we first saw it was Navestock Side, a common with grazing rights. It was kept close-cropped by goats and geese, and cricket had been played there more or less since cricket began. It became less interesting when the smallholders got grander ideas and started keeping cows, a prelude to giving up grazing anything at all, and the Side has now been relentlessly gentrified. The Green Man Inn, spoken of with bated breath because of the escapades of the Irish licensee's family and the horses they kept in the tumbledown stables, is now a port of call for passing motorists of eminent respectability.

Even more exciting than Navestock Side was Weald Park which came within our range when we had put nursery days and the pram behind us. It was the remnant of ancient and much larger hunting grounds, surrounding a splendid Tudor house sadly demolished since the last war. Part of it was a deer-park with herds of red and fallow deer enclosed within high fences, and the whole of it was strictly preserved for Mr Tower's excellent pheasant and partridge shoot. The Park had a footpath about two miles long from Coxtie Green, near us, to South Weald village, the first part through woodland and the rest, in the deer-park, over short turf nibbled by innumerable rabbits. The Squire's gamekeeper, who was indeed death to marauding dogs, was held up to us by the maids as a terrifying bogeyman and I firmly believed that if you put so much as one foot outside the clearly marked path he would instantly appear and do to you whatever was meant by 'Trespassers will be Prosecuted' on the numerous notice-boards. I only once saw him because he lived in a house deep in the woods but on this occasion he was in the post office. He wore a dark green corduroy suit with leather leggings and a gun over his arm; his elderly hatchet-face was fierce enough to justify his reputation.

There were many delightful places within a mile or two where you would find cowslips, not too common and one of the few wild flowers worth picking, mushrooms, blackberries or just dry turf where it was pleasant to sit in the sun in the solitude not easily found at home. As one grew older one could roam without question in the holidays as long as one came back in time for meals. We seldom saw a stranger and we knew all about bulls and the dogs to be avoided. There were many people working on the land and you were never far from someone who knew perfectly well who you were. The circumstances of private employment, and the extent to which everyone knew everyone, spun a shining web of safety for the children of the gentry.

Twelve

SPECIAL OCCASIONS

The most special occasion of a recurring nature was Christmas Day, when the house came to a climax of excitement and the frontiers were down between the departments and spheres of influence which had to be so carefully differentiated at other times. Sounds of merriment emerged from unexpected places, senior servants fraternized on each others' ground and allowed themselves to joke with their juniors. I can understand now something of the feat of organization it entailed for my mother and why she used to say drily that she never knew which was the longer, Christmas Day or the Fourth of June (on which Eton College celebrated George III's birthday). About the latter we might perhaps have sympathized because, during my brother's time there, most parents went by train and had to remain all day on location. For those like us, arriving at about noon and leaving after darkness and the fireworks, there were long spells of having nothing much to do. First, unless your relation was scholarly enough to take part in Speeches, there was watching cricket in which none of us was very interested. The housemaster's lunch could not be called exciting and was only too quickly over. Seeing the Chapel, the pictures in the Provost's Lodge, a school art exhibition and some more cricket occupied a long afternoon until the sumptuous tea, with strawberries, nobly provided by my brother in his approximately twelve by eight foot room. This had a bed which was swung up against the wall in daytime but must have been let down for us to sit on. Had we been sentimental we might have seen a certain pathos in the well-kicked desk, the shabby armchair and the few little pictures and ornaments brought from home to relieve the sombre aspect of the boyproof necessities provided by the housemaster for generations of boarders.

The whole day was punctuated by meetings between fathers who were old friends, or possibly enemies, and parents stood around talking so that we felt frustrated at not getting more quickly to our destination however little, in fact, we wanted to do so. We were in our very best dresses and straw hats, new and unfamiliar, giving rise to apprehensions that my brother might not be approving them. For him clothes were easy enough as he had only to wear his tidiest tails, white tie and top hat, and look as much as possible like all his schoolfellows apart from those infinitely superior beings, the members of Pop (the Eton Society), who sported fancy waistcoats and adorned their hats with sealing-wax. All the same it must have been an ordeal for him and the usual chaff between brother and sisters was frozen into monosyllabic glumness and agonizing self-consciousness. The parade of wives and children before old schoolfellows was undoubtedly one of the objects of this exercise and perhaps we sensed that we were under critical scrutiny from someone like my father's old fag or fagmaster. After all, parents were not all that old themselves. At last the moment came when the boats were marshalled for the daylight procession downstream to supper, and the oarsmen, including in due course my brother, appeared in their Georgian sailors' costumes, crowned by straw boaters decorated with ribbons, flowers and gilt crossed oars, far outdoing their sisters' party hats. After another long wait we gathered on the river bank for the return procession in darkness, illuminated by a magnificent firework display. The climax came when the boys 'tossed' their oars upright and stood up in their narrow eight-oared racing boats, or remained sitting in the ten-oared Monarch which contained some school heroes, such as the captain of cricket, who could not row at all. Sometimes a boat overturned and the Monarch was pretty well guaranteed to provide some thrillingly wobbly moments, the unaccustomed champagne at the supper and the hopping and skipping of fireworks all around no doubt contributing to the delicious precariousness of the whole operation.

It was assumed by everybody that we enjoyed the Fourth of June and probably it never occurred to anyone to question this or try to opt out. I know now that I did not enjoy it but I am glad to have been put through it because on these and other less exacting visits to Eton I absorbed the peculiar Englishness of it all, and the impression of this has remained with me. The splendour of Windsor Castle, St George's Chapel and School Yard were somehow not incongruous with the ritual mudlarking of the Wall Game played in the gloom of foggy

St Andrew's Days. It was something that belonged essentially to youth, boredom shot through with moments of exaltation, uncertainties and agonies of shyness, unquestioning family loyalty, and obedience to parental wishes however strange.

Returning to Christmas, my mother must have found the day long not from lack of occupation but from too much of it, and my relations' energy astonishes me. It would start for parents and grown-up guests with the early Communion service at 8 am, involving a sharp half-mile walk and return for breakfast soon after 9. The staff and children had been up even earlier and we would have been going over the contents of our Christmas stockings, which we had till we were about eleven. The long black woollen stockings, borrowed from Nanny, would be hung on the ends of our beds but must have been removed after we were asleep, filled and put back again. Such was my excitement that I hardly seemed to sleep at all on Christmas Eve but I must admit that I never detected the operation. I only half believed in Father Christmas but this did not prevent him terrifying me and if there was one at a party, giving out presents, I roared the place down until told who was under the disguise. 'It is only Mr So-and-so', my mother would call out, shattering for the sake of peace any illusions other children might have been harbouring. They probably believed he came down the chimney but my accident-conscious parents thought we might catch fire from looking up the chimney for him, so for us his reindeer sleigh kept firmly to the roads.

Stocking contents had a certain delightful sameness. At the toe would be a bright sixpence, rising later to half-a-crown and in special years a five-shilling crown piece. After that an orange to stuff out the foot, and the leg was filled with small objects which gave an exciting bumpy feel if one crept to the end of the bed to reconnoitre in the early morning. These turned out to be little tin toys, a clockwork mouse perhaps, a top, a box of chalks, furniture for the dolls' house or a miniature teddy bear. Two splendid crackers and a piece of holly stuck out at the top. Certain things were absolutely barred: nothing made of celluloid because of its terrible inflammability, no fireworks then or at any other time, and no sweets as we only had these, strictly rationed after meals, later on Christmas Day, and in Easter eggs. Some chocolate fingers once got into my stocking by mistake and I stealthily ate them. Children were often asked to show their tongues, for some medical reason, and remembering this I had the presence of mind to rub mine on a towel, thus transferring the telltale brown stain to an

Luncheon-party in the United Universities Club tent at Lords for the Eton and Harrow cricket match, 1929. F. Procter, Vicar of South Weald; Uncles Will and Douglas Pott; Jim and Bill; Lesley; Mary Grant; Kathleen; Joyce; Min Fane. Morning-dress for men and garden-party dresses and hats for women were normal for this event of the London social season, attended mainly by those with Eton and Harrow connections, but including non-cricketing families

Lunch at the Essex Hunt point-to-point races about 1931. Jim, on shooting-stick; Costick, the butler, not normally present at picnics, but there for the fun of it; Uncle Will Pott; Barbara; Kathleen; Joyce; Lesley; Mary, wife of Uncle Bertie Pott, who is on the right

Lawrence Silver Wedding Group, 1931, in the Italian garden at Pilgrims' Hall. The family are in relatively informal summer clothes, such as they would have worn on Sundays.

The outdoor and indoor staff, with Kathleen, Bill and Joyce, on the presentation to him of a clock on his twenty-first birthday. Back row: Charlie Sewell, gardener; Pollard, cowman; Sankey, handyman; A. Murrant, chauffeur/groom; Kathleen; Currell, gardener and farmhand. Second row: Fewell, gardener; John, footman; Puttock, butler; Tom Roscoe, headgardener and farm-manager; Bill; Alice Stubbings, head-housemaid, with the second housemaid; Charlie Lucking, groom. Front row: third housemaid; Joyce; kitchen and scullery-maid, Nellie Roscoe, dairymaid, M. Rapley (Nanny) and Mrs Wright, cook.

even more conspicuous place. However, miracle of miracles, no one noticed and I got away with something which there would have been a row about even on Christmas morning. Our teeth were a matter of great concern to our parents, but frequent and painful visits to the dentist, the ban on sweets and rigidly enforced cleaning night and morning with Calvert's pink powder evidently paid off as we have all kept our teeth into old age. The pulling of crackers, donning the paper hats which came out of them, the examination and comparison of our new toys went on until we managed to dress or were dressed in Sunday clothes.

At breakfast in the dining-room we had our first meetings and greetings with the grown-ups but apart from the glorious thrills of anticipation it was like an ordinary Sunday. Then the impatiently awaited moment for us to give our presents to the maids arrived at last. The recipients' pleasure can have been nothing to that of the givers but they played up very well, simulating all the required surprise at gifts which they must have seen in the making. The preparations had gone on for weeks because nearly all our offerings were of our own manufacture. We made cross-stitch kettle-holders, needlecases and penwipers with flannel insides covered with bright scraps of cloth or leather. We stuck wallpaper round tiers of match-boxes to make miniature chests of drawers. We spoilt perfectly good pencils by attaching tassels to them with blobs of sealing-wax. We sewed and painted and framed and stuck, going into the local town from time to time for any adjuncts which had to be bought out of our pocket money. Then we had the delightful experience of seeing the bill sent along and the change brought back in a little wooden ball which ran on rails across the ceiling of the shop. It seemed like magic because you could not see the person functioning at the far end of the rails. This all sounds rather idyllic but in fact our basically altruistic efforts were accompanied by much quarrelling, secretiveness or giving away of secrets, cribbing of ideas by the younger members and snubs from the elder ones, all rather pleasurable to us but dementing for grown-ups.

It was our first resident governess, Miss Gray, who started us on making things, at the age of about seven. She only stayed a year and long afterwards we heard that she was thought to be unkind to us and unduly repressive. This surprised me because I do not think we minded or even particularly noticed any severity and were not in the least afraid of her. We learned to get our knuckles quickly under the table when she whipped out the ruler to rap them but she seemed to think the warning enough and never pushed the matter further. On her lapel she wore a button from which her pince-nez eye-glasses normally hung. We knew we had to pay special attention when she pulled them out on the cord coiled up inside, and put them on her nose, but tension relaxed when she took them off and let them reel up again with a little whirr. She taught us how to knit and my brother and I both started on khaki scarves for the troops. His was better than mine which tapered oddly after the first three inches and was abandoned. We also did cross-stitch on coarse-meshed canvas, the usual pattern being brightly coloured diamond shapes outlined in black. Her favourite craft was beadwork and she taught us some simple forms but I have never known what she did with her own brilliant little squares, made of emerald or sapphire or ruby glass beads alternated with plain transparent ones. Beads themselves were fascinating things and one of my most memorable Christmas presents was a box containing several trays of them, the top one, divided into compartments of different colours, being visible through the glass lid. I could hardly bear to spoil the pattern by using them.

Our Christmas distribution only included the maids, the men's requirements, such as cigarettes, being too expensive for us. My parents gave joints of pork or beef to married men, probably money to single ones, and the maids usually had dress lengths to make up themselves. For the long skirts and sleeves of those days they must have needed about six yards. On the rather rare occasions when we had a Christmas tree in the afternoon these, as well as our own presents, would be piled round its foot but this made for an almost unbearable wait as well as a lot of extra work. A young fir tree would be cut down and fixed securely in a tub. A Father Christmas doll, kept for this purpose, would be attached at the top and the branches would be hung with paper chains which we had made ourselves, tinsel and glass balls. Small coloured candles, each on a little tin saucer with a clip, were fixed to the branches and quickly snuffed out if they looked like starting a fire, which they frequently did. This and the somewhat overwhelming effect of the whole house-party and staff being assembled at once, and perhaps feeling rather shy, made the tree somehow never quite the success it should have been.

According to our more usual routine we would have given the maids their presents after breakfast and then dressed for church. We wore a lot of clothes against the cold and these took a long time to get into. There were gaiters to be fastened with innumerable buttons needing a buttonhook owing to the stiffness of the cloth. One had to wait one's turn for this to be done as it was not really possible to do it for oneself. Then scarves had to be wrapped round and securely pinned, handkerchiefs and the collection coins put in our pockets and gloves produced at the very last moment so that we did not lose them before we started. They were knitted woollen ones until we graduated to lined leather or even rabbits' fur. The latter were an acceptable present though on the whole presents of clothes bored us. Church on Christmas Day was magical. Devoted parishioners had decorated it the day before, putting white chrysanthemums on the altar, holly and other evergreens over the font, on the window sills, at the foot of the lectern and round the pulpit. It would be packed and we had to share our pew with the neighbour who habitually used it for evensong, which hardly any of us ever attended. We only shared at Christmas, Easter and the Harvest Festival, and never saw her at other times for she was the horse-knacker's daughter, this sinister occupation rather setting the family apart from the community. The choir stalls were full of surpliced figures, the usual dozen or so small boys being reinforced by several men who turned out only for festivals, and if there was a boy with a good enough voice he would sing a solo in the anthem. We knew most of the boys and it was astonishing to see them transformed into these angelic beings.

We always stuck out the whole service. Not for us removal before the sermon which would have been both babyish and also horribly conspicuous. Stoically we forebore from scratching our chilblains, looking behind us, whispering or kicking the pew, and observed the veto on sharing hymnbooks, which was apt to start us giggling. We resented help with finding our places; although we were totally unmusical and hardly sang at all we sternly found our own or at least pretended to. At last the moment came to put our pennies in the bag during the final hymn and we could rush home for half an hour with our stocking presents before our simple lunch. In view of the evening feast to come we used to have cold ham and beef, potatoes baked in their jackets, stewed fruit for us, mince pies with flaming brandy for our elders and the Stilton cheese which only appeared on the sideboard at Christmas time. Food, however, was of little interest as the great moment of the day approached.

After lunch the presents were all arranged in individual piles on the floor and we danced round them hand in hand in a ring until at a signal each settled to his own pile. Some presents were inevitably known about beforehand but there were always surprises, especially from uncles and aunts, and sometimes we triumphantly achieved surprises for them. Unless it was a year for a really important present such as a bicycle our best things probably did not cost much over a pound, for which an astonishing amount could be bought. A child could not go much beyond five shillings for a parent, a little less for a brother or sister, uncle or aunt, and a shilling or sixpenceworth had to do for the rest. All presents, however, were quite genuinely paid for our of our pocket-money, tips and what could be earned from small tasks or growing radishes and mustard-and-cress for schoolroom tea. My brother of course was on a different footing, having to fend for himself at school, but I do not think I ever bought anything for myself until at the age of fifteen I acquired William Blake's poems in a charming edition for seven and six. The next thing was a pair of skates for eight shillings and sixpence and after that I slid quickly enough down the slippery slope of self-indulgence into the chronic impecuniosity of my generation.

The present-giving completed, the grown-ups sought rest or exercise and we went out for a walk with them or played our new games and read our new books in the nursery. For tea round the hall fire there would be a splendid iced Christmas cake decorated with little silver balls and a tiny fir tree or Father Christmas in the middle. We cannot I think have eaten much of it but it remained a standby throughout the holidays. Hitherto the day had largely been given up to the young but as evening approached the adults took over. We played some quiet games with them until it was time to dress, and how we dressed! Children in party frocks, fathers and uncles in tailcoats and white ties, mothers and aunts in shimmering evening dresses with bare backs and shoulders and a lot of jewellery. There might be a few old friends from outside, all equally magnificent, and we sat down about fourteen, a panic developing if anyone looked like failing and making the number thirteen. My parents were not superstitious but many people were and they did not want guests to feel uncomfortable. Dinner started with clear soup, followed by a stupendous turkey of about seventeen pounds, richly stuffed, surrounded by sausages and served on a huge plated hot-water dish. Then followed the plum pudding, brought in flaming with brandy, and there was always orange jelly for those who by now could take no more rich food. The jelly was special because it was poured into and set in the scooped out skins, tasting deliciously of fresh oranges, and a real stimulus to jaded appetites. Dessert was enchanting, with brightly coloured crystallized fruits which appeared only at Christmas, Elvas plums, almonds and raisins. Almost too excited to sleep, children were packed off to bed after this and the rest of the party probably ended up in the billiard-room after the port and coffee rituals. The staff, having performed these prodigies of effort for us, had their own turkey on Boxing Day. The family, apart from the children, were usually out hunting or shooting with a slab of cold plum pudding for lunch. The real treat for the servants, however, was soon after Christmas when they all went to London for lunch and a pantomime or musical comedy matinée. This was a very grown-up party and they never told us much about it but we would be entertained for quite a time with snatches from something like *Chu Chin Chow* or some fairly robust jokes from the pantomime.

From the memoirs and biographies now appearing it is evident that the twenties and thirties were a great time for parties, and this rubbed off on the children. The sub-teenage kind, usually held in the winter, was planned around tea, starting at about 3.30 and ending towards 6.30. We would arrive in the brougham, much muffled up, and I remember intensely disliking a white knitted shawl of open weave which was added to everything else. It had the abhorred quality of babyishness, being just like the ones used in prams and, like the baby, always smelling slightly of sick and of wool washed with soapflakes. When unpeeled from all our coverings we would be propelled into the room to meet our hostess, parted from the grown-up who had brought us and left uneasily taking stock of our twenty or so companions until some game was started. As we did not go to school there were few other children whom we knew well or were pleased to see. However, the inhibitions were soon broken down by a game of Musical Chairs, its variation Musical Bumps, played with cushions instead of chairs, or Hunt the Slipper. The latter involved sitting in a ring on the floor with one person concealing a slipper. This was shuffled rapidly from one to the other and the child in the middle had to try and guess where it was and pounce upon it. If he captured it he sat down in the ring and the person guilty of losing the slipper took his place. The game was popular and fairly rough, with much squeaking from ticklish girls who were apt to get the slipper entangled in their frilly skirts.

Blind Man's Bluff was all right too, usually starting off with a blindfolded grown-up who made a great play of catching one of the children who milled around him. There would be a thrilling moment when he tried to tell by feel whom he had caught, and no doubt he prolonged the suspense by guessing wrong a few times. Once the child was caught and correctly named that one in turn was blindfolded and so it went on until all who wanted had had a turn. This worked out quite well because only a few ever wanted to be 'he' in any game and so attract attention to themselves. The majority eschewed such exhibitionism but were thankful when someone came forward and put the rest out of danger. The least popular games were those in which willy-nilly you might be made conspicuous, as in the abominable Forfeits in which, if you failed some test, you might be compelled to kiss another child, something which in real life you never did if you could possibly help it. Hide-and-Seek was the best of all, in which everyone hid except one 'he' who had to go on till he caught somebody. There were, however, only too few families who would allow their guests the run of the whole house, so that you could get under beds and into coat-cupboards and hide so effectively that you sometimes had to give yourself up for fear of being forgotten altogether. One magnificent Tudor house had a range of bedrooms opening out of each other, many disused and dark, gloriously terrifying.

For the hostesses, no doubt, tea was the big effort and very beautifully they used to get it set out. Around Christmas time there would be crackers, always one beside each plate and others in the middle for random activity after the first organized round when we crossed arms in a ring and pulled all at once. They were made of crêpe paper in bright colours, edged with gold or silver paper lace, and always had a cut-out scrap stuck to them. More beautiful still and probably much more expensive were those which had an under-layer of coloured paper screened by a transparent film which we used to call 'gelatine'. These crackers, being brittle, pulled better than the others so that the cardboard strip with its explosive charge went off instantaneously and less frighteningly than when extracted from the outer wrappings and pulled in its bare state by big bold boys. Every cracker contained a paper hat and a 'motto'. This was a little printed slip carrying a riddle, an aphorism or a joke which was often a little bit off-colour. Grown-ups enjoyed reading these out to each other and no doubt saw points which escaped us; we did not find them interesting though I can remember a few to this day, such as, 'Why does an old maid wear gloves?' Answer, 'To keep away the chaps.' The better crackers held little toys as well as hats, a whistle, a charm or, best of all, pieces of gimcrack jewellery set with glass gems.

Tea was usually and preferably fairly plain, a wise precaution because children, probably having a less well-balanced diet than today and often made to eat too much, were fatally liable to be sick if excited. I was a martyr to this failing myself as well as getting hiccups if I laughed too much. However, if you could stick to thin bread-and-butter, with or without jam, sponge fingers and dry biscuits, all was probably well. Robuster types could tuck into chocolate icing and rich plum cake. Often there was an entertainer after tea. This might be a conjuror or a ventriloquist. Rabbits were produced out of top hats, baby chickens out of people's ears and skeins of coloured silk handkerchiefs out of nowhere, to the accompaniment of what seemed excruciatingly funny patter. Ventriloquists were not quite so popular as conjurors as there was often a rather distasteful sentimentality, or soppiness as we called it, between the performer and his doll, and you really could always see that he was making the sounds himself. A Punch and Judy show was a rarity and rightly so as the gruesome knockabout terrified some of the weaker vessels, producing screams and floods of tears.

My parents made history by finding a charming puppet show, its elaborate stage being rigged in the drawing-room bay. The proprietor was one Arthur Gair Wilkinson, a gentle red-bearded artist who would make a little money from his performances and then spend it going to Italy to paint. His characters must I think have been based on those of the *commedia del'arte*; the simple stories they enacted were full of whimsical humour, innocent romance, nobility and pathos such as to bring tears to the eyes. It was rather above the heads of small children but older ones, such as I then was, were entranced and so were the grown-ups. Anyone not appreciating the finer points could, however, get a lot of fun lying on the floor to see up above the curtain where Mr and Mrs Wilkinson manipulated the strings and did the talking. It was a huge success.

As we grew older the time shifted from tea to an early supper, with cold chicken, jellies and fruit salad, and we would play prepared games with a competitive element such as identifying advertisements, or follow clues for a treasure hunt or act Dumb Crambo and charades, preferably with the aid of a dressing-up box. In the former, one side mimed words which the others had to guess and in the latter the actors played little scenes in which each syllable of the chosen word, and finally the whole of it, were worked or dragged into the conversation for the audience to spot. Gradually we progressed to dances, which we did not mind so long as they were not cotillions. With these, favours were distributed and you had to look for the person who had the matching or complementary one and thus became your partner. Parents praised these parties and indeed the favours were always pretty and ingenious, but most children thought it affected and were rather glum about it. I am ashamed now to remember how little some of us helped to make parties go but it is undeniable that the companions held up to us as examples of good manners and co-operative behaviour seldom turned out so well as the others, and some came to really bad ends.

Apart from formal parties we quite often went out to tea or had others to tea with us and being only about six in number we then played quite different games. Children still play many of them but it is so teasing to read of old-fashioned games without having a clue as to what they consisted of, that it is perhaps not superfluous to describe some of them. Among card-games there was Old Maid in which a Queen was extracted from the pack and put aside before dealing. Everyone then discarded any paired cards, such as two eights, two knaves, and so on, and then, starting from the left of the dealer, each player took a card from the fanned hand his neighbour held out to him. If it made a pair in his hand he could discard, and gradually some players would drop out with all their cards paired. The single Queen, however, remained odd and the spectators and the last few players would hold their breath as someone managed to pass on the fatal card or pair all his own. Finally someone was left with her, and cries of 'Old Maid' went up. Snap was a game of many variations, played with an ordinary pack or with specially designed cards. They were dealt out equally and you went on turning out one at a time in front of you until you matched an opponent's, whereupon the first to say 'Snap' took all the cards which the loser had out in front of him. Eventually someone got them all from everybody but it could go on a long time with fortunes constantly changing. A variation was Smiling Grab in which you were supposed to stare your opponent out in complete gravity when a pair turned up, and this always produced fits of giggles in all but very resolute grown-ups. With Donkey, sets of four cards of similar denomination, one set for each player, were separated from the pack, shuffled and dealt. On a word of command each player passed one card on and picked up another until someone got four of a kind, on which he quietly put down his hand. The last to notice that he had done so and drop his own had to take one letter of the word Donkey until somebody had got the whole word spelt, a game in which someone lost but no one won. Racing Demon was for two or more players, each with a complete pack. They set out their cards in front of them in sequence, red five on black six and so on, and used them to build up on the aces which both would put out in the middle as they turned up. The cards needed to build on the aces were often covered, and you would watch in a frenzy while your opponents roared ahead and your vital four of hearts or whatever was hopelessly frozen under a black three until you could get that out on an ace of spades or clubs. The winner was he who managed to be first in getting all his cards out on the central aces, and the contest waxed fast and furious. A much quieter twosome was Beggar-my-Neighbour in which two people divided the pack and played the cards out one by one, each having to give his opponent four for an Ace, three for a King, two for a Queen and one for a Knave. Eventually after several narrow shaves in which a penal loss was saved by a lucky Knave with only one plain card to be paid for him, one player would get the whole lot.

An immortal game played with special cards was Happy Families, the pack consisting of sets of four composed of Mr Bun the Baker, Mr Soot the Sweep, etc, their wives and two children, Miss and Master. This reminds me, incidentally, that the domestic staff, except Nanny and the nurserymaid, addressed us children as Master or Miss so-and-so and spoke of us like this, except no doubt among themselves when they would use the simple christian name. Until a few years ago there were still a few people who always called me Miss Lesley, regardless of marriage, but of these old friends none remains now. However, to return to Happy Families, the object was to make up as many complete sets as possible until all the cards were used up. Each player, when his turn came, asked for some character in one of his own potential sets from the person he guessed might have it. If he was wrong the turn passed to that player who would then put his own question, in the traditional words, 'Is Mr Bun at home?' to be answered perhaps, 'No, Mr Bun is *not* at home.' In case of a favourable response the card had to be handed over and the enquirer got another turn repeatedly until he enquired unsuccessfully. By a process of elimination and deduction the players soon got to know where the wanted cards were but one mistake could cost you all your partially completed sets, a bitter moment for small children and calling for the utmost self-control. Another very popular game was Up Jenkins. Three or four people would face a similar team across a table and on the words 'Up Jenkins' from the captain of one side the other would slam all hands palm downwards on the table, concealing a sixpence somewhere under them. The coin might immediately be seen, poking out between fingers, or a fatal chink might betray all, but if there was no sign the order 'Creepie-crawlies' might be given and fingers would have to be 'walked' over the table. If the sixpence was still undetected the same side hid it again, but otherwise it changed over, and the score of each side was kept until everyone had had enough.

Parties became more enjoyable as one grew older, either because one knew the other guests better or because one actually got to like meeting new people. There would be dances for about twenty couples in private houses and they had a formality which was reassuring rather than otherwise. Girls wore dresses which when I first grew up were short in the skirt but very long in the waist, if you could call it a waist. These became interchangeable with what the mesdemoiselles in Paris called 'robes de style' with full skirts down to the ground, and in the thirties this more attractive type of dress took over altogether. For girls there was still a convention called 'coming-out' when, with or without being presented at Court or having a dance of your own, you were invited to grown-up parties and, with great kindness on the part of the neighbours, included in small gatherings to work off your gaucherie. You learned what a lunchtime cocktail could do to you and that if you kept the rule of not speaking with your mouth full you would never get enough to eat.

The début frontier was not drawn nearly so definitely as in our mother's day; she would have pinned up her hair, hitherto worn long, and would have lengthened formerly short skirts. In my day you were as likely to have your hair cut off for a 'shingle', cropped at the back and waved over the head and ears, as to pin it up in plaits and buns. Skirt lengths remained what you had been wearing for some time as did your daytime clothes generally. Young men had attained, for the evening, to the uniformity of dark suits or, at any time after the age of sixteen, black dinner-jackets with black ties. No longer did the Christ's Hospital boys clump round in stout buckled shoes, blue gowns tucked into their leather belts to display yellow stockings; or small fry wear the wide turned-down starched collars, waist-length black jackets and striped trousers of the Eton suit, by no means exclusive to Eton. Nearly all had white kid gloves, whether or not they put them on, and gravely and politely entered their names and their partners' in the little cardboard programmes with dangling miniature pencils which were provided for all but the most informal affairs. We circled decorously in foxtrots, one or two-steps, sometimes an old-fashioned waltz, until, growing more boisterous in our advancing years we took to gallops and polkas and uproarious sets of 'Strip the Willow', a country dance in which couples in turns came from the ends of two rows to perform some steps in the middle. Dances in private houses usually began at about 9.30 and ended around 2 am, but hunt balls and the like, in public assembly rooms such as the Shire Hall, would start at 10 and might go on till 4 am. Whatever time we got home, however, we were expected to put in a reasonably punctual appearance at family breakfast next morning. My youngest sister kicked over the traces about this, said she did not want breakfast and got away with it.

These social activities were interspersed with local functions such as school treats, and garden fêtes held for good causes. The biggest one ever undertaken at my home must have been the Peace celebrations of 1919. Our big flat lawn, the fields with gates conveniently opening on to a main road, the stock of ropes, ladders, hurdles, stakes, tarpaulins, nets and sacks inseparable from such an establishment were exactly what was needed. All kinds of relatively unfamiliar things were brought in, such as screens and poles for coconut shies; boards with holes through which you hoped to bowl two or three balls to win a pig; a huge marquee for teas; and trestle tables for games of skill and chance. The band from the nearby Poplar Schools arrived to provide the music, much of it of a patriotic variety, and was sat down under one of the big chestnut trees. These London boys, either orphans or taken away from bad homes, wore a smart uniform of scarlet jacket, blue braided trousers and a pill-box cap on the side of the head. Accompanied by their cheerful music the local schoolchildren were marshalled and paraded in front of our whitebearded clergyman to receive a mug with a bag of sweets in it. We did not get the sweets of course but I have my mug to this day, a rather coarse white pottery affair with, on one side, the flags of Britain, France, America and Italy arranged round a globe with a dove over it and, on the other, a dove between the words Peace and Justice. At private parties we were under pretty close supervision, but on this occasion no one had much time for us. We were given a little spending money and left to roam, going into the house sometimes for rest and refreshment. There were sack-races for which you put your feet into the corners of farm sacks and waddled towards the winning post as best you might. In the potato races you picked up a row of six, one by one, returning to base each time, and the egg and spoon race was run with wooden spoons and china eggs out of the hen-coops. It was a gloriously fine day of seemingly endless bliss but at last shadows lengthened, the prizes were distributed, numbers thinned, and the Poplar boys shook the spittle out of their trumpets for the last time and went off in their waggonette. It was a day meant for children to remember and there must be many of us who still do.

Thirteen

SOME ORDINARY THINGS

There has been and still continues a dispersal of Edwardian and neo-Georgian artifacts perhaps comparable to what would have happened if Goths had descended on a Roman villa, taken away the odd bits of loot they fancied and after a few years started selling them in far away places to people who admired them but had never seen them in use. Nothing quite so sensational has happened here and the purpose of most things now to be seen in antique or junk shops is usually fairly obvious. Indeed in a few houses, some open to the public, some not, much of the old routine is still kept up. Yet the continuity between early twentieth-century culture and the things which went with it is far more fragile than might appear. The resident domestic staff who sustained it belonged to a tradition which had been streamlined, refined and liberalized but still consisted of personal service as rendered for centuries by poorer people to those rich enough to employ them. In the process the employees evolved their own rules and skills, made them seem indispensable and created a vested interest in their upkeep. It was an industry which embraced those who worked for and those who supplied the needs of upper and middle-class households and there was an informal but well-recognized trade union with its own codes.

The real change came with the introduction, over a very short period, of sophisticated domestic technology accompanied by political and sociological changes which made personal service on the former scale unnecessary and indeed undesired on both sides. The result has been that many objects needed in a large household either have been converted to other uses or have found their way on to the market. The whole context in which they were used and the relationship between people and things depends on living memory. The most prolific diarists and letterwriters seldom go into sufficient detail for a complete reconstruction, and archaeologists know that deductions, seemingly convincing at the time, may turn out to be wildly astray. You have to be at least seventy now to remember anything much of the finest flowering of Edwardian culture which has been dying a lingering death ever since 1914. Even my sisters, born four and seven years after me, are frequently surprised at some of my early memories.

The catalogues of the Army and Navy Stores, Victoria Street, London, from its foundation in 1871 until the series was discontinued in 1939, are invaluable as an aide-memoire and highly evocative. Originally a co-operative society for officers and the official classes generally, it offered middle-of-the-road goods for middle-of-the-road prices, and as much of its trade was done by post an enormous number of objects was illustrated by line drawings, which in non-fashion articles changed surprisingly little over the years. Our abominable travelling nursery bath, for instance, was still available in 1935 though by then it had been relegated to the camping section. (The catalogues are now very rare but the 1907 one was reprinted by David & Charles as *Yesterday's Shopping*, and although now out of print it can be seen in or requested from public libraries.)

I note that the japanned and brass cot in which I got my head stuck was described as a drop-sided one, and it was always kept dropped after that incident. As it was meant for a three- or four-year-old child, who should have known better, the rather large gaps cannot have been seen as a hazard, but the first cot to which the baby was promoted after the basinette had more safely spaced flat oak rails. The basinette had a foundation of basket-work but it was entirely covered in frilly muslin, beautifully lined in soft cotton material, had a draped canopy at the head end and was adorned with satin ribbon bows, blue for a boy and pink for a girl. It was relatively portable, the precursor of the 'Moses basket' or carry-cot, but normally rested on its own white enamelled iron stand.

The appointments of the writing-table were important and also attractive. Few houses, at least in the country, had telephones before the 1914 war and even if you had one other people did not. The writing of letters and notes was a major industry and there would be several different kinds of paper in the drawers or in a stationery-case. The best quality was thick, in white, grey-blue, a vivid pale blue, or the 'Silurian' greenish-grey speckles. The surface was beautifully smooth and your pen slid easily over it. The address was die-stamped at the head in black or blue and the shop where you bought it kept the die to use on new supplies when you ordered them. Ordinary printing was only considered suitable for letters to tradesmen, but sometimes a home die-stamper, which embossed the address without colour, was kept for informal use. Some people, though never us with our very muted tastes, had elaborate letterheads with a picture of a little puffing engine against the name of a station, or a telephone against a number, and envelopes with a crest on the flap. When I was young a lot of people used black-bordered paper when in mourning and my grandmother, a widow of many years' standing, never used anything else. The black edge could vary from almost a quarter-inch to a thin line and I do not know whether this betokened the degree of relationship or whether, as with clothes, you gradually began to brighten things up. Grown-ups deduced a lot from writing-paper and paid particular attention to that on which the characters of servants were written by employers. Scent was absolutely damning, mauve was not considered at all good and inverted commas round the name of a house spoke volumes to them. Any fancy touches such as deckle-edges were distrusted.

Penholders came in many attractive forms. My mother's favourite one was a silver-mounted procupine quill, very light and thin, and she used a J nib which made thick down strokes and lighter upward ones. We children had Relief ones, less exacting for an unformed hand and taking up less ink. In old people's houses you sometimes saw a real quill pen, as opposed to a feather penholder, made for use rather than ornament from the greyish turkey or goose feathers which looked shabby but were best for writing with. Illuminators continued to use them for a long time and some possibly still do, putting a penknife to its proper purpose for shaping a nib and cutting its writing edge sharp and thin. Whatever pen you used you would get an inky second finger, and a piece of pumice stone was kept in the bathroom for cleaning it. Ink was nearly always blue-black but purple was not uncommon if old-fashioned, associated in my mind, for some forgotten reason, with emotional elderly ladies. Green and other colours were not approved of generally but children were of course unaffected by these taboos. We wrote blithely in ink of all colours on delightful paper with little pictures at the head. These lightened the painful task of getting the thank-you letters done after Christmas and birthdays.

As they wrote so much most people wrote rapidly and used a lot of blotting-paper, which could retain the mirror image of a whole page.

Blotting-paper, white or speckly-pink, therefore had to be renewed frequently and cutting the large sheets to the right size was a job for the schoolroom. There were many blotters throughout the house because each room had one and guests used to retire to their bedrooms to write letters, or at least gave this as an excuse for a little rest. Few people, unless known to be delicate, would actually own to lying down during the day. In case your hostess did not provide writing materials your dressing-case probably contained a small blotter as one of its fittings.

The contents of a lady's fitted dressing-case vividly suggested the customs of the time. If one pursues the archaeological simile one might expect an early twentieth-century site to be littered with as many hairpins as the ubiquitous potsherds. Women shed them copiously in spite of the ingeniously kinked shanks which should have held them in place. Black, bronze or white, they came in many strengths and sizes, from the tough straight ones, resembling miniature croquet hoops, through the medium kinky ones to the so-called invisibles made of very fine wire and intended to secure stray wisps. For travelling they would be put into one of the dressing-case jars. The big ones were used for fixing the horsehair pad which was the foundation for the fashionable piled-up hair-do. Even my mother, who had plenty of hair of her own, wore one of these for years, and secured the main tresses to it.

No doubt there were circles in which make-up was freely used but it certainly was not in ours, and the flasks and jars contained eau-de-cologne rather than scent, and cold cream as a general lubricant. People who suffered from chapped hands carried glycerine. I had never seen or heard of a foundation medium until I went to Paris and then my room-mate and I dashingly bought the smallest-sized tube of Pond's Vanishing Cream, which we shared. This was a great advance because the powder stuck to our noses and we need not so often squint down with one eye to see if they had acquired the shine which was so much frowned-upon. Manicure of an inconspicuous kind was provided for, with scissors, a file and adjuncts for polishing rather than varnishing. Tweezers were included on the same fitted board, and a penknife. The latter, I suspect, was used on corns which, owing probably to pointed shoes, were very prevalent among women. Children learned very quickly not to tread on anyone's feet as this was apt to produce a yelp of agony and a brisk cuff from the best-tempered of adults. Many elegant feet were undoubtedly studded with corn-plasters.

An indispensable tool was the pair of glove-stretchers of bone or ivory, looking rather like tongs but acting in reverse. With these you stretched the fingers of the beautifully made fine kid gloves worn for all well-dressed occasions, day or evening. These were never cheap and, as they were not the same after dry-cleaning, emitting, especially if your hands were warm, a disagreeable smell of cleaning fluid, you took great care of them. They split only too easily if you forced your hands into them but if you bought a comfortably large size they wrinkled inelegantly. So you carefully inserted the stretchers, squeezed the handles so that the blades opened inside the fingers, and dusted in a little talcum powder before putting the gloves on. If you had a maid or were being fitted in a shop you put your elbow on the table or counter and held up your hand while the glove was smoothed over it. The stretchers had another rougher use, for the pale yellow chamois leather gloves used for riding and country wear generally. These were washed in soap flakes and the soap left in so that they dried very hard. You rubbed them soft and stretched the figners so that they became almost as good as new, and a pair would last for years.

In the kitchen garden of my old home you might still see, for I saw it not many years ago, our old hip-bath being used to soak pot plants in. It was relegated to this purpose in the early 1930s, when the senior staff became sufficiently broadminded to allow the footman to come upstairs and use the maids' bathroom at stated times instead of having his bath in front of the pantry fire. It was brought into the house again during a shortage of hot water in the great freeze-up in 1939, the first year of the war, and we then appreciated its virtues. As the butler said, it only took one can of water to cover the bottom and though he blushed, and we for him, at the unpremeditated double-entendre, we saw exactly what he meant. These hip-baths are by no means uncommon objects even now but I doubt whether many people appreciate the elaborate ritual of using one before the days of bathrooms and a handy water-supply. Its shape is curious, with a high sloped back, a shallow saucer about three feet across for the water and little flat lobes on each side. These must, I think, have been designed to help with handling as they are too low for arm-rests and not needed to hold soap or sponge as you are so near the floor anyway. A full-grown person reclined with feet outside, the term hip-bath therefore being quite accurate.

Though economical in water, the allowance probably being a two-gallon can to fill it and another to top up with, the bath was far from economical in labour. The cans were the big brown ones which always gave out a strong smell of paint when filled with hot water, and they were very heavy to carry. Whoever brought them had also to lay down a big thick bath mat on which they and the bath stood, preferably in front of a bedroom fire. The very fastidious or draught-conscious might require a screen to be set up round it and in any case the towel-rail or its big brother the clothes-horse would be moved over to stand near. And then when you had finished the bath had to be carefully emptied into slop pails and carried away to drain somewhere.

The heavy work attached to coal-scuttles was done by the footman, who carried them to the rooms, and the houseboy who filled them outside. I am reminded by the Army and Navy catalogue of how many kinds there were and how many examples we had. In the dining-room and drawing-room there were hods of bright steel from which large bits of coal would be extracted with tongs. There was also a wooden box with sloping front which held a separate zinc liner containing very small coal or slack, as we called coal-dust. This was used for slowing down the fire for an hour or two when no one would be in the room. In the schoolroom we had one of these and also a brass scuttle which went with the fender and fire-irons, all this bright metal taking on the flickering reflections which added so much to the cosy appearance of the room. This scuttle was of a kind of helmet shape and you could, though people seldom did, lift the whole thing by the handle and shoot coal from it straight on to the fire. The best bedrooms had the wooden zinc-lined type and the nursery had the same design but of black japanned iron instead of wood, with brass mounts which the nurserymaid used to polish. Also highly polished was the brass on the fireguard of stout close wire mesh, between two and three feet high, which was kept hooked to the sides of the chimneypiece so that it could not be pulled over. As well as brass round the top it had an extra rail on which small objects were hung to dry or air. Nannies had a horror of damp socks, which they regarded as absolutely lethal, and they liked to air anything they had been ironing. Undoubtedly things did get damp in cupboards and drawers to an extent now forgotten by those who live in centrally heated houses and with plenty of electricity or gas.

The beautiful cleanliness and fragrance of the house was maintained by a rigid daily and weekly routine conducted under the eye of highly trained upper servants. Dusting, sweeping, kitchen scrubbing, the cleaning of bathrooms, washstands and sinks were done every day and there was a less frequent rota for turning out rooms. This expression meant what is said; moveable furniture would be put out in the passage while carpets were thoroughly brushed, woodwork and parquet surrounds polished. Spare bedrooms, after turning out, were kept muffled in big white cotton dustsheets and you would have thought did not need much preparation when needed. Unexpected guests were not approved of, however, probably because mattresses really did need airing. If they fussed unnecessarily about some things our elders were right about the dangers of damp beds. The room would therefore be opened up at least two days before, a fire lit in the winter and two or three stone hot-water bottles put among mattresses and blankets. Beds were never left made up so sheets and pillow-cases came ready-aired from the linen cupboard.

Our ironing board was both heavy and ricketty so that ironing was usually done over a folded blanket and old sheet on the nursery table. In the winter the flat-irons could be heated in the nursery grate but in summer they had to be fetched up from the kitchen. They were very, very hot and the whole procedure was carried out with great deliberation. For some reason no one liked the bright metal shoe which could be sprung on over the iron to avoid dirt, and the iron was usually rubbed on emery paper when taken out of the fire. Spitting was taboo in the nursery and no one would have set us so bad an example but elsewhere the heat of the iron was tested by spitting on it. If the spittle ran quickly into a little ball and instantly disappeared the temperature was about right but in spite of all precautions ironing was usually accompanied by the smell of scorched cloth. Things were rolled up damp to keep in some moisture before ironing but if any more were needed water was sprinkled on very skilfully with the fingers from a bowl. This was preferred to any sprinkling devices such as I am sure must have been available.

In spite of all the routine care the annual spring-cleaning was regarded as a necessity. It lasted about a fortnight and took place in May when no more fires would be needed. My parents removed themselves, usually to a walking holiday somewhere in England, but the children generally remained for at least some of the time, and would have missed a lot of fun if they had not. Some of the men from stable and garden used to come in and out to help with moving heavy furniture, taking up and taking out carpets to be beaten or washing paint in high and awkward places. A carpenter or plumber might be required for some job found to be necessary and all the chimneys had to be swept. There would be a lot of cheerful banter between the men and the maids, between those on the top of step-ladders and those holding them steady, and though curtains were sometimes dropped on people's heads and buckets overturned nothing seemed to matter very much.

Huge consignments of curtains, loose covers and bedspreads would be despatched to Pullars' of Perth for dry-cleaning, miscellaneous basic upholstery of armchairs and sofas being then exposed to view. Sometimes long-lost toys reappeared, there were unfamiliar things to play with and there might be the major excitement of finding a mouse's or bird's nest which had miraculously escaped the housemaids' daily onslaught. It was extraordinary what a difference the annual spring-cleaning made to a habitually well-kept house. The opening of doors and windows for a good blow-through with curtains removed probably had much to do with it and it was perhaps not purely fancy that furnishings put out of doors on a fine sunny day retained some of the scents of the garden. The air really felt as though it had been renewed, and newly cleaned paint, lamp-fittings and picture glasses retained their sparkle until fires started up again in the autumn.

Our house was ill-placed in regard to services. Neither gas nor electricity came our way but went east and west of us to where there were more users. This deprived us of various labour-saving devices which must already have been commonplace but our lack of main drainage was by no means so unusual. It was a subject one did not hear discussed but there must have been a series of soakaways and cess-pits before the ultimate destination of the sewage in a noisome ditch and swamp two or three hundred yards from the house. If there had been any serious health risk from this it would no doubt have become apparent in the half-century we were there and we probably suffered much more from the house-flies and blue-bottles breeding in farm and stable, and the innumerable mosquitoes swarming off our many delightful ponds. Small children were devoured but adults became either more resistant or less attractive to the pests and were not troubled. Effective insecticides or the scientific knowledge to apply them were perhaps lacking, and the only remedies were swatting and sticky papers for the flies and Pond's Extract for the mosquito bites. This was also the specific for bruises and there was something very comforting about the astringent smell of witch-hazel added to the attention that went with it.

We were probably no more hypochondriacal than other families but we seem to have suffered a good deal from minor ailments such as would probably now be dealt with by more effective drugs, left to be grown out of or prevented altogether. The flies must have been the cause of our frequent internal upsets and these were treated by the doctor, usually with a medicine having a thick white sediment, probably bismuth. If not afflicted in this way we were constipated, or were thought to be going to be; or else the grown-ups had transferred to us their anxieties on their own account, the trouble apparently being universal. The mildest measure was California Syrup of Figs, and if that was not strong enough then calomel overnight, chased by Eno's Fruit Salts next morning. For themselves our elders seemed to favour senna pods or the romantic-sounding cascara sagrada. We had frequent colds in the head with such accompaniments as earache, sore throats and obstinate coughs, occasionally calling for the use of the steam kettle. This had a long spout with a fan-shaped mouth, was heated on the spirit stove normally used for the babys' feeds, and put near the patient in a tent made over the bed with sheets. A temperature only slightly above normal kept us in bed for what we felt was an inordinately long time. In between colds we were given various supposed tonics and body-builders, including Scott's Emulsion of cod-liver oil, from the bottle with a label showing a fisherman shouldering a fish as big as himself, and Byno, whose label said something about phosphates. Childhood is all very well but there is much to be said for the established health, completed growth and unbroken skin of adult life.

As the great duvet revolution looks like engulfing us all it may perhaps not be superfluous to look back at the beds of my youth. The curtained four-poster only survived as an anachronism or an affectation as it does today, but beds were on average a good deal higher then. There was no attempt to disguise them although there must already have been such things as sofa-beds for bed-sitting-rooms, and older children, the cook or a lady's maid in a house like ours would use their bedrooms to sit or work in. The distinction, however, remained, that you knocked on bedroom doors but never on those of sitting-rooms, it being assumed, so our governess told us, that no lady would ever be doing anything in the drawing-room which she would mind someone catching her at. Beds always had heads and slightly lower feet of brass or iron, japanned iron and brass, or polished wood. The brass ones were elaborately made and the balls which adorned the corners were made to screw on and off, a fact quickly discovered by small children. This kind, however, was beginning to go out of fashion, so while Nanny had a rather grand white and brass bed the ones in the front of the house all had wooden ends. Our own and the maids' were of iron without any brass. A special kind of joint kept the side pieces rigidly at right angles to the ends but enabled the frame to be taken to pieces for storing or moving.

Most beds had a wire mesh foundation with some spring in it on which the mattress was laid. The best were stuffed with horsehair, which itself was springy, but there were also cotton-flock ones, liable to become lumpy. All kinds were firmly buttoned through at intervals of about eight inches to keep the stuffing in place, and they were usually covered with harsh linen or cotton ticking in black and white, or brown and fawn stripes. Very good quality beds, particularly the excellent ones sold by Heal's in Tottenham Court Road, had a box-mattress as foundation instead of the wire mesh, and this was about a foot deep. It contained a number of upright spiral springs confined in ticking and over it would be laid an ordinary hair mattress. The modern interior-sprung mattress is a combination of the two and has tended to lower the height of beds. To cover the inelegant ticking there would be a valance or frill hanging down all around and this would match the general scheme of the room though it was seldom of the same material as the bedspread.

When the bed was made an old blanket was laid on the mattress and the undersheet firmly tucked in all round except at the head where it was wrapped over a bolster, a cylindrical pillow stuffed with firm feathers and covered in ticking. Over this came one or more softer, rectangular pillows, those in the best rooms having dazzlingly white pillow-cases with hem-stitched or frilled borders. The top sheet was folded over two or three blankets at just the right height, about halfway up the pillow, and the whole lot tucked in. Then came an eiderdown with a very light filling covered in thin silk or glazed cotton and ventilated at intervals by small stitched holes; these were important and if they were obliterated in a re-covering the quilt was never the same again. The bedspread was usually put over the eiderdown in the daytime and fashions in these changed. In my time one only saw the heavy white honeycomb ones, or lace, in rather humble homes or lodging-houses, and silk or brocade ones were for grander use. The only patchwork quilts or covers one ever saw were genuine cottage ones. Beds were usually on small casters and did not move easily so making them was a job for two people and very companionable, conducive to a comfortable gossip. The proper turning down of beds was a point of honour in well-ordered households and was usually done while the family was at dinner. A maid would take off the bedspread, open one corner invitingly and, in cold weather, slip in a hot-water bottle round which she had wrapped your nightdress. Now let us imagine getting between beautifully ironed shiny linen sheets under fluffy blankets and the most superior kind of eiderdown in the best spare-room, on the right side of that brass-studded door shutting off the nether regions inhabited by the footman, maids and children, the dog and Jazz, the kitchen cat.

EPILOGUE

On page 98 I wrote 'A space behind this door allowed for a little courtship of the maids, unobserved or at least ignored by the cook and, in one case at least, ripening to a long and happy marriage.'

Many years later some verses were written for this couple, Alec and Betty Stanley, by a friend at Pilgrims' Hall who knew them in old age. From what they told her she composed the following tribute, presented to them at a party given for them by the Pilgrims' Hall community on their departure for New Zealand in 1989, sixty years after Alec went to the Lawrences as gardener. The Miss Brown of Dytchleys who paid for Alec's bicycle is one of those remembered on page 110 for their kindness and good works.

Patricia Garratt's verses are a spontaneous testimony to the human side of the strictly ordered régime I describe in my book and I welcome them as matching my own memories of the privileged end of it. They are therefore printed as one of the happy endings from those days long ago, with grateful acknowledgement to the author.

To Alec and Betty

We gather here this evening with a mixture of emotion,
To say 'Farewell' to well-loved friends as they fly across the ocean.
Their thoughts are of the future, yet memories thick and fast
Will doubtless keep on flooding back with pictures of the past –

The school at Bentley Common was where Alec – just a lad –
Gave Ben Cooper, his Headmaster, all the grey hairs that he had!
Then, out to work at Dytchleys, where he did a full day's job
And earned himself a 'fortune': his weekly wage, nine 'bob'!

He wore out much shoe leather as he walked to work each day,
No doubt with great imaginings on what to spend his pay!
Miss Brown came to the rescue, and to Alec took a liking:
She gave to him a crisp pound-note and the chance to change to biking.

And so to 1929. From Dytchleys now he parted.
He rose then to the dizzy heights, for at Pilgrims' Hall he started!
Now God up in His Heaven had very quickly spied
A very lovely kitchen maid who'd make a pretty bride!

Her name, of course, was Betty, and she would stand each day
Just gazing from the window at the lad across the way.
She watched him in the garden as he worked with all his might.
She went to bed elated and dreamt of him all night!

The romance grew in secret, and few were 'in the know'.
It was aided by the house-boy taking letters to and fro.
Then Alec popped the question, and Betty's dreams came true:
Not just a kitchen full of veg, but a handsome husband too!

The Cottage then became their home, and for fifty years or more
They've loved and raised a family there, had an ever-open door.
They've lived through war together, when Alec did his part
And fought for King and Country – signing-on right at the start.

While Betty spent her efforts for the young evacuees:
Bringing love to many children with such gentle expertise.
Returning then from Hamburg, back to Pilgrims' Hall again,
Alec wore a trodden pathway from the Cottage in Back Lane:

'til he came to his retirement in 1968,
When he put away his hard-worked tools and closed the garden gate.
He left a place of beauty that still abides today:
He'd tended it with sense of pride and care in every way.

He still comes on occasion to look with endless joy
At all he can remember of his times here as a boy.
So as we close the curtain on memories close to you:
No doubt we each have others that we will treasure too.

So now, Alec and Betty, we each would thank you here
For joy you've brought to all of us, and thoughts that we hold dear.
May God grant you His blessings in everything you do,
May life there in New Zealand be very sweet for you.

Patricia Garratt

INDEX